# CASH VALUES

# CASH VALUES

MONEY AND THE EROSION OF MEANING
IN TODAY'S SOCIETY

*Craig M. Gay*

WILLIAM B. EERDMANS PUBLISHING COMPANY
GRAND RAPIDS, MICHIGAN / CAMBRIDGE, U.K.

First published 2003 as part of the New College Lectures Series by
University of New South Wales Press Ltd
University of New South Wales, Sydney NSW 2052 Australia

This edition published 2004 by Wm. B. Eerdmans Publishing Co.
2140 Oak Industrial Drive N.E., Grand Rapids, Michigan 49505 /
P.O. Box 163, Cambridge CB3 9PU U.K.


Printed in the United States of America

10  09  08  07  06  05        8  7  6  5  4  3  2


**Library of Congress Cataloging-in-Publication Data**

Gay, Craig M.
    Cash values : money and the erosion of meaning in today's
    society / Craig M. Gay.
        p.        cm.        — (New College lectures)
    Includes bibliographical references.
    ISBN 978-0-8028-2775-3 (pbk.: alk. paper)
    1. Capitalism — Religious aspects — Christianity.
    2. Money — Religious aspects — Christianity.
    I. Title.   II. Series

    BR115.C3G38    2004
    261.8′5 — dc22
                                                  2004047170


www.eerdmans.com

# CONTENTS

# FOREWORD

by Trevor Cairney
Master, New College UNSW

Money is something to which much is attributed – good and bad: 'You won't solve the problem till you throw some money at it.' 'Money means power!' 'Money is the root of all evil.' It seems that all of life is affected by money or its pursuit. Hence, as a topic, the role that money plays in our world is a highly relevant one. It was for this reason that Associate Professor Craig Gay from Regent College, Vancouver (Canada) was invited to present a series of lectures on the topic at New College (UNSW) during August 2002 as part of the New College Lectures.

The New College Lectures are an annual series of public lectures delivered in New College on the campus of UNSW. They provide an opportunity for an eminent scholar or practitioner to take up some aspect of contemporary society and comment upon it from the standpoint of their own Christian faith and professional experience. The Trustees of the Lecture series decided in 2001 that capitalism would be an ideal topic as a focus for the 2002 Lectures. Craig Gay was chosen as one well qualified to make comment. Dr Gay is an Associate Professor of Interdisciplinary Studies at Regent College in Vancouver Canada. He has a Bachelor of

Science degree from Stanford, a Diploma in Christian Studies and Master of Theological Studies (Regent) and a PhD from Boston University in Religious Studies. His many publications include the highly relevant *With Liberty or Justice for Whom? The recent evangelical debate over capitalism.* As a scholar he has spent much of the last 15 years examining and writing about the theological and ethical implications of capitalism and modern technology. This is a book that raises many questions: Is free market capitalism as bad as some people suggest? Is it synonymous with greed, selfishness, oppression and exploitation? Or, at the end of the day, has it been an effective economic system? Is there a relationship between capitalism and technological innovation? Is money the only way to measure value or is it simply a tool that has become the major 'denomination' of value in our world? You will be pleased to know that the book also attempts to offer some answers as well as questions. However, above all, it will open up conversations about these complex matters that cannot adequately be addressed in a single book. Those who see themselves as Christians will find the final chapter particularly thought-provoking as it attempts to bring biblical frameworks to bear on this important topic. I commend Associate Professor Gay, both for providing a stimulating series of public lectures, and also for offering us this excellent book that will continue the conversations commenced at the 2002 Lecture Series. New College is also grateful to UNSW Press, and in particular to Robin Derricourt, for making this publication possible.

# PREFACE

I was delighted to be asked to give the 2002 New College Lectures. In addition to being impressed – and humbled – by the intellectual stature of previous New College lecturers, I was thrilled to have an excuse to make my first trip 'down under'. We'd had a number of Australian students at Regent College over the years, and time and again I'd been intrigued by their pluck and self-deprecating humour. What kind of place, I wondered, could produce such consistently appealing people? Well, after only a brief visit, I'm still not sure how to answer this question, but our experience of 'fair dinkum' Australian hospitality has left us itching to go back. Hopefully we'll get another crack at that whip some day soon!

To preface what follows, I need to comment briefly on my choice of topic. I also need to thank many of those who helped me prepare the lectures as well as the book you have in hand.

The invitation I received in the Spring of 2001 suggested only that the lecturer take up some aspect of contemporary society and comment upon it in the light of Christian beliefs and values. As it happened, the invitation arrived shortly after I'd given the concluding lecture for a new Regent College course that I had titled

'Christianity and the Economic Order'. The course attempted to provide students with a brief history of economic analysis, an overview of the political-economic ideologies that have prevailed over the last century, and some discussion of the theological and ethical implications of global capitalism. The gist of the course was simply to suggest that if we are going to make the best of the economic situation we find ourselves in today we'd better begin by trying to understand where the modern market economy has come from and just how it functions.

Along this line, I had noticed that *money* seemed to lie at the intersection of almost all topics we covered in the course. It seemed to be the hub from which any number of spokes extended and around which much of the contemporary world seems to turn. Money, for example, is crucial to the objectification and rationalisation of modern economic action; the 'making of more and more money,' as Max Weber put it, is the '*summum bonum*' of modern capitalism's distinctive ethos; and the flow of money around the world today is an essential aspect of the process of 'globalisation'. Money also appears to be directly or indirectly related to many of the more perplexing 'cultural contradictions' of modern capitalism, not to mention to some of the more perplexing personal problems many of us face individually.

Add to this the fact that the use and abuse of money has quite frequently been addressed both by the authors of scripture and by many notable figures in the Christian tradition and, clearly, *money* – and particularly the way money functions within modern capitalism – is an aspect of contemporary society deserving of Christian reflection and comment.

I was very pleased, therefore, when the trustees of the New College Lectures agreed to allow me to lecture on the topic of money. I was also pleased to have an excuse to return to the work of the master theorist of the role that money plays in modern society, Georg Simmel.

I would like to thank a number of people for their help with the project: Alan Beavis, former Master of New College, for inviting me to give the 2002 New College lectures; my research assistants, David Allen and Debbie Erickson, for gathering materials both for the Regent College course as well as for the lectures; Professor Trevor Cairney, Master of New College, and his staff for graciously hosting us during our stay in Sydney; my friend Kurt Shaefer, Professor of Economics at Calvin College, for carefully reading and commenting insightfully on an early draft this book; Karen Wuest and Claire Sauer for their editorial acumen; and Robin Derricourt and Mary Halbmeyer of UNSW Press. And, as always, I would like to thank my wife, Julie, and our four children – Andrew, Elsa, Owen, and Nicholas – for being patient with me as I worried my way through this project, as well as for being wonderful and intrepid travelling companions. And finally, I want to thank my dad, Henry M. Gay III, for a great many things, but particularly in the present context for modelling the kind of gracious lightheartedness that is, I believe, the only posture that can, before God, prevent our money and possessions from taking possession of us. *Soli Deo Gloria!*

# INTRODUCTION

> In the global economy that is still emerging, the power of money
> and the institutions built on it will supersede that of any nation,
> combination of nations, or international organization now in
> existence.
>
> Jack Weatherford, *The History of Money*[1]

In a recent best-selling analysis of the process of globalisation
entitled *The Lexus and the Olive Tree* (1999), *New York Times* edi-
tor Thomas Friedman asserts that the 'driving idea' behind the
international system that has effectively supplanted the Cold War
since 1989 is 'free-market capitalism'.[2] Advances in telecommuni-
cations technologies, the development of information networks,
and what Friedman terms the 'securitization' of debt instruments,[3] have led to an 'inexorable integration of markets, nation-
states, and technologies to a degree never witnessed before'.[4] This
unprecedented integration, he contends, is not an economic fad,
and it is not a passing analytical trend. Rather, global capitalism
is a social fact that will have consequences that reach far into our
future.

The global capitalist system, Friedman stresses, operates on the basis of a series of rules that enjoin opening, privatising, and deregulating national economies for the sake of making them both more competitive as well as making them more attractive to foreign capital investment. The more you allow market forces to rule, Friedman writes – describing the economic regimen he terms the 'golden straightjacket' – and the more you open an economy to free trade and competition, the more efficient and prosperous your economy will be and the more political stability and material comfort your country will enjoy as a result.

Within the context of an increasingly global market, in other words, technological advances in production, transportation and communications have, in effect, given individual and institutional investors a 'vote' in the management of economic, political and social conditions all over the world. As these investors value long-term economic growth – and as growth hinges upon political and social stability, freedom from arbitrary political interference, and the ready availability of information – they will tend to vote *for* countries that manage their internal affairs in a responsible and more or less open fashion and *against* countries that do not. Countries that inspire the confidence of global investors through the proper management of economic, political and social conditions will thrive. Countries that fail to inspire such confidence will not.

The key theorist for understanding the global capitalist system, Friedman asserts, is the economic historian Joseph Schumpeter.[5] 'The fundamental impulse that sets and keeps the capitalist engine in motion,' Schumpeter observed, 'comes from the *new* consumers' goods, the *new* methods of production or transportation, the *new* markets, the *new* forms of industrial organization that capitalist enterprise creates.'[6] Indeed, the dynamic of capitalism is such as to relentlessly replace the past with the present, to unravel tradition in the interests of innovation and growth, and to 'destroy' the status quo for the sake of what will come next. The fitting term that Schumpeter coined to describe this process is that of 'creative

*designed obsolescence?*
*planned*

destruction'.[7] Friedman echoes Schumpeter's insight: '[T]hose countries that are most willing to let capitalism quickly destroy inefficient companies so that money can be freed up and directed to more innovative ones will thrive in the era of globalization. Those that rely on governments to protect them from such creative destruction will fall behind in this era.'[8] And not only will the latter fall behind economically, but their governments will also face increasing pressure internally to do whatever it takes to get into the global capitalist game.

There will, Friedman admits, be sources of 'backlash' against global capitalism's golden straightjacket. Politicians will resist surrendering power to foreign corporations and international regulators; religious leaders will resist globalisation's 'creative destruction' of local religious customs and traditions; environmentalists will protest global capitalism's apparent depletion of the earth's resources; and many will resent the fact that global capitalism will inevitably prove relatively more profitable for some than for others.[9] But Friedman also predicts that there will be a backlash against this backlash. 'With all due respect to the revolutionary theorists,' he writes toward the end of his analysis:

> the 'wretched of the earth' want to go to Disney World – not the barricades. They want the Magic Kingdom, not *Les Miserables*. And if you construct an economic and political environment that gives them half a sense that with hard work and sacrifice they will get to Disney World and get to enjoy the Magic Kingdom, most of them will stick with the game – for far, far longer than you would ever expect.[10]

Friedman's contention that free market capitalism is what currently 'drives' the process of globalisation is perhaps debatable. Other theorists would place more emphasis upon technological and/or cultural developments, and not without justification.[11] Yet Friedman's analysis does suggest that global capitalism is a social fact that we need to take very seriously, and it raises a number of interesting – if not exactly new – questions: Is the spread of free market capitalism around the world a good thing or not? More specifically, how can Christians think *Christianly* – which is to say theologically – about global capitalist development? And, finally, how should we think about our own participation within the capitalist system?

These are the sorts of questions I attempt to answer – or at least begin to answer – in this short study. I will be working from a number of classical and contemporary sources in an attempt to elucidate what capitalism is, how it works, and what sorts of material and cultural influences we can expect it to have, both upon us and upon anyone else who decides to get into the global capitalist game. Admittedly, this is an almost absurdly ambitious task. Modern capitalism is an enormous and immensely complicated phenomenon, and the reader should not expect to find a comprehensive treatment of it in the following pages. Still, it is my conviction that if we would respond to global capitalist development insightfully and redemptively, we need to try to understand how it functions and why. Along this line, it seems to me that many of capitalism's contemporary critics misunderstand its essence – commonly assuming it to be simple greed – and that this misunderstanding renders their criticism somewhat wide of the mark, if not altogether obtuse. Of course capitalists can be greedy, but so can anyone else as, for example, Schumpeter observed: 'Pre-capitalist man is in fact no less "grabbing" than capitalist man. Peasant serfs for instance or warrior lords assert their self-interest with a brutal energy all their own. But capitalism develops rationality and adds a new edge to it.'[12]

The 'new edge' to which Schumpeter refers has to do, I will assert, with capitalism's use of money, that is, with capitalism's 'exaltation of the monetary unit',[13] to use another one of Schumpeter's clever phrases. Money's objective and mathematically manipulable 'denomination' of value is the grist for the mill of modern economic computation. Its deft conversion of things and qualities into specific quantities provides the 'price signals' necessary for free market capitalism to operate. Money is what makes economic rationality possible. Along this line, I will contend that the 'objectification' of value made possible by the use of money lies very nearly at the essence of modern capitalism and is absolutely crucial to its remarkable and unprecedented productivity. Modern capitalism's inventive use of money, I will contend furthermore, far transcends those uses to which money has traditionally been put, which is why I have chosen a new term, the Money Metric, to describe it. Basically, money has become one of the most important 'measures' in the determination of 'value' in the contemporary world. Indeed, the very nature of worth is increasingly understood today simply in terms of the value of money, which is to say, in terms of 'cash values'. Money, like the mechanical clock, is one of the key instruments of the modern age.

And yet it is this very key – this objective 'denomination' of value made possible by the use of money – that seems to lurk just beneath the surface of many of the perplexing social and cultural problems so often associated with modern capitalist development. I will discuss a number of these problems at some length, but suffice it here at the outset simply to note that the 'monetisation' of value, a procedure that the market economy puts to very good use, entails a remarkable degree of *imposition*. After all, the 'nominal' values we attach to things by means of the abstraction we call money do not necessarily reflect – and may actually obscure – their real or intrinsic value. Furthermore, when our imposition of monetary values upon things is combined with modern science's 'objectification' of nature, we are actually tempted to doubt that there *is* such a thing as intrinsic value. Rather we are enticed into believing that values are simply human designations and that 'value', like beauty, simply lies in the 'eye of the beholder'. This, I will argue, is a very significant problem, particularly from a religious point of view. For surrendering ourselves to this temptation obviates the religious imperative to look beyond our own designations of 'values' for *real* value. It renders us increasingly insensible to the inherent qualities of life and to the real beauty and *giftedness* of being. Indeed, resting content with the imposition of merely monetary values upon all things can ultimately render us insensible to the goodness and graciousness of God.

And so I have come to believe that capitalism poses a paradox for Christian ethics and involves us in a genuine dilemma. It poses a paradox in the sense that it exhibits seemingly contradictory qualities. On the one hand, modern capitalism is historically the product of *Christian* civilisation. Precisely because it is the product of Christian civilisation, capitalism fosters and can be justified in terms of a number of basic Christian values, not the least of which is Christianity's concern for the material well-being of people and for individual freedom. 'Of all the systems of political economy which have shaped our history,' Roman Catholic thinker Michael Novak writes in an insightful apology for the market system, 'none has so revolutionized ordinary expectations of human life – lengthened the life span, made the elimination of poverty and famine thinkable, enlarged the range of human choice – as democratic capitalism.'[14]

Novak is surely correct in his assessment. And yet modern capitalism is also one of the principal carriers of the insidious process of secularisation.[15] It fosters a kind of 'practical atheism' and conveys a subtle nihilism that empties the world of substance and enervates moral reasoning. As Irving Kristol noted a number of years ago in a study entitled *Two Cheers for Capitalism*, 'The enemy of liberal capitalism today is not so much socialism as nihilism. Only liberal capitalism doesn't see nihilism as an enemy, but rather as just another splendid business opportunity.'[16] Or, as Kurt Eichenwald put it more recently in the *New York Times*, 'a staggering rush of corporate debacles is raising a disturbing question: can capitalism survive the capitalists themselves?'[17] The answer, Eichenwald concludes, is that it almost certainly will 'if only because survival is the most profitable outcome for all involved'.[18] Perhaps he is right, but it seems to me that we would do well to consider the possibility that the assessment of profitability alone is not really equal to the task of disciplining capitalism's creative destructive process.

The contradictory aspects of modern capitalism are such that the path of least resistance for Christians has often been either to condemn the system outright or to vigorously defend it. Yet neither response is particularly fruitful. Condemning capitalism, while perhaps making us feel better about ourselves, accomplishes very little under contemporary circumstances. The global capitalist system continues to plough ahead in spite of this criticism, and its critics have no clear idea of what they would replace it with anyway. Defending the free market economy, on the other hand, blunts the prophetic edge and makes it seem as if Christianity's announcement of the Kingdom of God has actually only been a kind of exaggeration and that the 'Magic Kingdom' is really the best that we can hope for after all.

And so modern capitalism involves us in a dilemma in the sense that the market system – like modern science and technology, liberal democracy, and any number of features of our fallen culture – forces us to dwell in the awkward space between rash criticism and undue defensiveness. We cannot really avoid participating in and being implicated within capitalism's 'Money Metric', but as Christians we can seek to act redemptively within it. Indeed, we *must* seek to act redemptively within the system if we would strive to obey the commandment to love God and to love our neighbour. Doing so, however, will require us to carefully discern the source of the system's benefits as well as the source of some of its more serious costs, and this is what I aim to do in the following chapters. In the first, I will discuss the sources of capitalism's remarkable productivity. The news about capitalism in this first chapter will be mostly good, for it is indeed an astonishingly productive system. In chapter 2, I will explore the cultural and psychic 'costs' of capitalism's reliance upon money and 'price signals' in the determination of human purposes and values. This news about the market system will be largely bad, for monetary values, which are simply supposed to represent real values and preferences arrived at by other means, have a way of actually determining our preferences and becoming the *only* values. Finally, in chapter 3, I will outline a kind of theological riposte to the market economy's commodification of value, all the while encouraging us to be grateful to God for the system's extraordinary productivity. The critical theological question we face, I will suggest, is whether or not it is still possible for us to fit capitalism's remarkable productivity within a system of meanings and values that entirely transcend pecuniary valuation. Such a system needs to enable us to take economic productivity seriously for the sake of our neighbour, but it also needs to inspire us to be sincerely generous with each other. Finally, it would need to enable us to be 'lighthearted' with respect to money and possessions for the sake of our souls. Thankfully, the Gospel of Grace provides us with just such a system.

# SOURCES OF CAPITALISM'S
# REMARKABLE PRODUCTIVITY

Advanced industrial capitalism has generated, and continues to generate, the highest material standard of living for large masses of people in human history.

Peter L. Berger, *The Capitalist Revolution*[1]

As recently as a couple of hundred years ago life expectancy at birth was only between 30 and 40 years, and prior to the year 1400 it was only between 20 and 30 years.[2] In large part this was because only every other child prior to the year 1400, and only three or four out of five prior to the year 1800, lived to celebrate their fifth birthday. But, of course, they probably did not have much to celebrate with, for as recently as 200 years ago the vast majority of people in the world went hungry most of the time. In pre-industrial Britain, for example, one harvest in six was a complete failure, and even when there happened to be food most people were still crippled by a variety of dietary deficiencies, as well as by constant outbreaks of bacterial stomach infections from the consumption of rotten or poorly prepared foodstuffs. Personal and public hygiene were execrable; chronic and wasting diseases such as malaria and tuberculosis were endemic; and the relatively short lives of our ancestors were often cut even shorter by viral or bacterial infections such as cholera, smallpox, diphtheria and plague. There were almost no medicines and few effective cures for even the most elementary of medical conditions.

In short it was not that long ago – indeed, just a couple hundred years – that our ancestors lived amid conditions that we would consider appalling today. 'If we take the long view of human history,' Nathan Rosenberg and LE Birdzell, Jr observe in *How the West Grew Rich: the economic transformation of the industrial world*, 'and judge the economic lives of our ancestors by modern standards, it is a story of almost unrelieved wretchedness.'[3] The typical human society, Rosenberg and Birdzell note, has provided only a relatively small number of people with a humane existence, while most people lived in the abysmal poverty that has been the normal condition of most people throughout human history. We tend to forget the dominating misery of other times, they write, 'in part by the grace of literature, poetry, romance, and legend, which celebrate those who have lived well and forget those who lived in the silence of poverty'.[4] The past is often mythologised and bygone eras are often remembered as golden ages of pastoral simplicity, but in fact they were not. Most of us would not have survived long enough to become interested in a book like this, and the few of us who might have survived would, in all likelihood, not have enjoyed the leisure time to read it – and we probably would have been unable to read in any case.

We have come a very long way. As of the year 2000 most people in the world could expect to live into their mid-60s and many even into their 70s and 80s.[5] Astonishing advances have been made both medically and in terms of public and private hygiene. Infant mortality has fallen by more than 50 per cent in both developed and developing countries.[6] Incomes have tripled in both industrialised and developing nations over the last 50 years.[7] Many more people around the world have much more to eat,[8] are better educated,[9] enjoy more leisure,[10] and possess more consumer goods than ever before.[11] In particular, those of us in the West are, for the most part, prosperous, well-fed, healthy, well-educated, and quite astonishingly, comfortable relative to our ancestors. As Rosenberg and Birdzell go on to observe:

> [D]uring the last two hundred years there has come to Western Europe, the United States, Canada, Australia, Japan, and a few other places one of 'history's infrequent periods when progress and prosperity have touched the lives of somewhat more than the upper tenth of the population... In England, the United States, and parts of Western Europe, it became evident early in the 19th century (and later in other countries of the West) that an unusually high proportion of people were becoming better fed, healthier, and more secure than in the ancient Middle Eastern, Indian, Chinese, Greek, Roman, and Islamic civilizations – that is, *than at any other time in human history.*[12]

And in spite of a few notable exceptions, western-style prosperity and security continue to spread around the world today, lengthening life spans, reducing the incidence of fatal or disabling diseases, improving living conditions, expanding literacy and education, and enhancing privacy and personal choice.

It is true, as Rosenberg and Birdzell point out, that this remarkable transition from widespread poverty to generalised affluence did not occur overnight but developed gradually over a period of several centuries, basically as economic growth just managed to exceed population growth.[13] And it is also true that this transition has yet to occur for many of the world's poorest. Yet considered over the long span of human history, the transition from poverty to generalised prosperity has been sudden and dramatic, and it calls for an explanation. After literally millennia of almost universal poverty, western – and more recently a number of non-western – nations have managed to break free from it. How have they managed to do this?

A number of hypotheses have been forwarded to explain this remarkable transition to generalised affluence, some attributing western-style prosperity to various kinds of misconduct, such as slavery, colonialism, imperialism and the exploitation of labour. Yet as Rosenberg and Birdzell observe, all such hypotheses are plagued by rather significant empirical difficulties. They simply do not explain the facts of western development. In the first instance, *all* human societies have been characterised by the inequality of wealth and income but only a very few of them by sustained economic growth. It is the latter, then, that begs for the explanation and not the former. And western economic development has not been nearly as labour-intensive as theories emphasising the exploitation of labour suggest. Similarly, theories emphasising colonial exploitation fail to explain why certain colonies – notably the United States, Canada, Australia, New Zealand, Hong Kong, Singapore, etc. – seem actually to have benefited from the arrangement, while others – notably those in Africa – did not. Such theories also fail to explain why a number of nations – most significantly the United States – have managed to grow without colonies. For those nations that did hold colonies, furthermore, there does not appear to be any empirical correlation between the periods of colonisation and those of economic growth. In short, theories attributing western prosperity to misconduct of various kinds – as attractive as they perhaps are for other reasons – have simply not been able to explain the economic data.[14]

Other theories seeking to explain western development have emphasised the importance of western science and technology. Yet while science and technology have obviously played, and continue to play, an extremely important role in western economic development, scientific and technological progress cannot, in and of itself, explain how and why the West managed to grow so rich relative to other civilisations. After all, China and the Islamic nations were actually far more advanced scientifically and technologically at the beginning of the modern era. And the simple transfer of advanced technology from the First to the Third World more recently has not, in and of itself, led to sustained economic growth.[15]

Perhaps those of us in the West have simply been lucky. Perhaps we have simply been the beneficiaries of a series of historical accidents. Although we are undoubtedly fortunate, theories attempting to explain western economic growth in terms of chance events fail to explain why the West has been so *consistently* lucky, particularly over such a long period of time. As Rosenberg and Birdzell point out, the West has experienced one economic 'revolution' after another, e.g. the Mercantile Revolution from the 15th to 17th centuries, the Industrial Revolution of the 18th century, a second Industrial Revolution at the end of the 19th century with the introduction of electricity and the internal combustion engine and, most recently, the revolution in communications and information.[16] The odds against such revolutionary developments happening in the same places and to the same people by mere happenstance are long indeed.

Some other dynamic has obviously been at work in the West – and increasingly in the East as well – that has somehow led to a significant increase in sustained economic productivity. Rosenberg and Birdzell's contention along this line is that the West grew rich because political pluralism and the relative flexibility of western institutional life created the social 'space' requisite for entrepreneurial activity to emerge and flourish. 'Our general conclusion,' they write, 'is that the underlying source of the West's ability to attract the lightning of economic revolutions was a unique use of experiment in technology and organization to harness resources to the satisfaction of human wants.'[17] Rosenberg and Birdzell call this potent synthesis of experimental technology and economic organisation geared towards enhancing material welfare the West's 'growth system'.[18] The key elements of this system were the broad distribution of the authority and resources necessary for innovation; the lessening of political and religious restrictions upon innovation; and the simple incentive in the fact that the widespread economic use of a particular invention had the potential to make its inventors quite wealthy.[19] The West's growth system yielded innovations in trade and in the discovery of new resources, in production techniques, in organisation, as well as to the introduction of new products, particularly products intended for mass consumption. 'In the three-cornered relations of technology, the experimental economy, and growth of material welfare,' Rosenberg and Birdzell write, 'the experimental economy served as a more efficient link between science and growth than any other society had achieved, and the economy was itself the source of much of its own technology.'[20]

However *normal* the practical pursuit of improving our material circumstances may seem to us today, it is important to stress that such pragmatic practicality has historically almost always been subject to some kind of religious discipline, for the harnessing of resources 'to the satisfaction of human wants' has almost always been – as, indeed, it still is – subversive of social order. Hence Rosenberg and Birdzell's conclusion begs the question of why the social 'space' that seems to have opened up in the West beginning in the 15th century was allowed to fill so quickly with inventors, entrepreneurs, and other *practical* people who appear to have been principally concerned with material life, or – as Rosenberg and Birdzell put it – 'a social class with the capacity to effect innovations, with incentives or motives for innovation, with a source of ideas for innovation, and with immunity from interference by the formidable social forces opposed to change, growth, and innovation'.[21] Where did these early 'movers and shakers' come from? How is it that they were allowed to so revolutionise European society and culture?

## WEBER'S THESIS

This, of course, is the question Max Weber sought to explicate in his celebrated essay 'The Protestant Ethic and the Spirit of Capitalism'.[22] Weber saw that the West's growth system could not be explained simply in terms of technical or organisational developments – as important as both were – but that the modern system was animated by an unusual *spirit*, a disciplined yet supremely *practical* disposition towards material life.[23] The practical disposition, Weber noted along this line, had historically only managed to surface sporadically during periods of religious 'disenchantment', that is, during relatively brief interludes when religious understanding temporarily lost its ability to police the pragmatic pursuit of material interests. The fact that so much of modern social life – and particularly modern economic life – is shaped by practical and pragmatic concerns, then, would seem to indicate that something is shielding it from religious criticism. Either practicality has somehow received the sanction of modern religious understanding, so that what appears to be purely pragmatic and egoistic behaviour is actually religiously motivated in some way; or religious understanding has somehow been debunked within modern culture in such a way as to give a free reign to practicality and pragmatism. Weber's intriguing contention was that both are, in fact, true of modern economic culture, and that the former gave rise to the latter.

Weber argued that, at a particular juncture in western history, practicality became ethically significant within a fundamentally *religious* conception of the world. Indeed, Weber's central thesis was that it was the *ethical* rationalisation of the world wrought within Calvinist Protestantism – that is, the belief that the world *should* be actively reshaped to conform to the revealed will of God – that gave rise to an essentially new kind of practical outlook, one that was profoundly inquisitive and acquisitive, and yet that was also disciplined and rational and suspicious, as he put it, of 'the spontaneous enjoyment of possessions'.[24]

Weber attempted to capture the gist of this new and supremely practical spirit in the term 'worldly asceticism'. It was, he stressed, the combination of limited consumption with the release of aquisitive activity that first gave rise to practical and rational capital accumulation. And Calvinism's – and particularly

Puritanism's – uniquely practical, disciplined, and this-worldly spirit would not simply animate early capitalistic economic development, but it would also stimulate early modern scientific development. Indeed, it would eventually result in the practical rationalisation of all of modern life. 'As far as the influence of the Puritan outlook extended ...', Weber insisted, 'it favoured the development of a rational bourgeois economic life. ... It stood at the cradle of the modern economic life.'[25]

Calvinism's powerful synthesis of ethical duty and practicality appears to have been both intentional and unintentional. It was intended to the extent that it followed from the Protestant repudiation of the medieval distinction between 'sacred' and 'secular' work in the world. This meant that Protestants were more comfortable in affirming everyday work in the world than their Roman Catholic counterparts who tended, theologically speaking, to view work only as a kind of necessary evil. Indeed, the Reformers insisted that all practical activity in the world – or at least all practical activity not otherwise at odds with the moral law – was not only religiously legitimate, but was also to be considered an essential aspect of Christian obedience to the divine *calling*.

For Lutherans, the radical social implications of this new understanding were mitigated by the fact that Luther only envisioned the callings against the traditional backdrop of the late medieval social order. The practical and worldly aspects of the work entailed in one's calling were also consistently relativised over and against 'the life to come' in Lutheran understanding.

Calvinists, however, appear to have unleashed the radical social and economic potential of the Protestant redefinition of calling by insisting that the Christian is called to the deliberate and energetic *reform* of the social order itself such that it may be brought into accord with Holy Scripture. Practical, instrumental rationality was held to be crucial to this reform process. This, according to Weber, is what explained the curious admixture of otherworldliness and utilitarianism in Calvinist ethics:

It seems at first a mystery how the undoubted superiority of Calvinism in social organization can be connected with this tendency to tear the individual away from the closed [traditional social] ties with which he is bound to this world. ... But God requires social achievement of the Christian because He wills that social life shall be organized according to His commandments, in accordance with that purpose. ... For the wonderfully purposeful organization and arrangement of this cosmos is, according to both the revelation of the Bible and to natural intuition, evidently designed by God to serve the utility of the human race. This makes labour in the service of impersonal social usefulness appear to promote the glory of God and hence to be willed by him.[26]

Calvinists, in other words, tended to be somewhat more pragmatic than their Roman Catholic or Lutheran counterparts in assessing the actual results of economic actions. If something worked and was useful, it was deemed Christianly acceptable. The Christian was not to be bound by moribund tradition in economic matters but was instead expected to be open to practical and rational innovation in the service of his or her neighbour and in the interests of the common good.[27] Richard Baxter's late 17th-century advice is commonly cited in this connection:

If God shows you a way in which you may lawfully get more than in another way (without wrong to your soul or to any other), if you refuse this, and choose the less gainful way, you cross one of the ends of your Calling, and you refuse to be God's steward, and to accept His gifts and use them for Him when He requireth it: you may labour to be rich for God, though not for the flesh and sin.[28]

Weber also believed that Calvinism's synthesis of practical and substantive rationality was partly accidental. Indeed, one of his more contentious suggestions was that the utilitarian character of Calvinist ethics was a kind of unintended by-product of pastoral advice aimed at lessening the anxiety aroused by the doctrine of double-predestination. Such advice apparently affirmed that dili-gent work in the world was the best remedy for this anxiety, espe-cially if one's work revealed itself to be consonant with God's purposes by effectively advancing the common good. Weber noted:

> The religious believer can make himself sure of his state of grace either in that he feels himself to be the vessel of the Holy Spirit or the tool of the divine will. In the former case his religious life tends to mysticism and emotionalism, in the latter to ascetic action; Luther stood close to the former type, Calvinism belonged definitely to the latter. The Calvinist also wanted to be saved *sola fide*. But since Calvin viewed all pure feelings and emotions, no matter how exalted they might seem to be, with suspicion, faith had to be proved by its objective results in order to provide a firm foundation for the *certitudo salutis*. It must be *fides efficax*, the call to salvation to be an effectual calling.[29]

Weber went on to suggest that this emphasis upon effectual calling devolved in practice into little more than the belief 'that God helps those who help themselves'.[30] Yet it was this belief, he felt, that interpreted the tremendous diligence with which subse-quent generations of Calvinists sought to reform this worldly exis-tence by means of diligent, practical effort. The Protestant ethic thus proved to be a very powerful catalyst of social change and innovation, particularly in the economic ambit.[31]

The practical and pragmatic quality of the West's growth sys-tem thus appears to be linked, at least initially, to a number of Protestant theological innovations. Chief among these were the Protestant redefinition of the notion of Christian calling, a redefi-nition that affirmed secular work, as well as the revision of theo-logical anthropology such that the human task in the world was not simply to admire it but rather *to reshape the world practically for the glory of God*. Rather than expecting values to somehow inhere in the things themselves, Protestants displayed a nominalist readi-ness to assign values *to* the things of this world on the basis of an external standard. Of course, the standard was initially that of the holy scripture, as well as effectiveness in serving the common good. As Puritanism devolved into Deism during the 18th century, however, *pecuniary* success eventually came to serve as a kind of proxy for both.[32] Indeed Weber observed that the great religious epoch of the 17th century had bequeathed to its utilitarian successor in the 18th 'an amazingly good, we may even say pharisaically good, conscience in the acquisition of money, so long as it took place legally'.[33] The *summum bonum* of the Protestant economic ethic, Weber went on to insist, was, quite simply, 'the earning of more and more money, combined with the strict avoidance of all spontaneous enjoyment of life'.[34] The ethos of early modern capitalism, in short, was not simply free from the past, but it was prepared to completely rethink traditional values, to reassign them, and to restate them in entirely new – and largely *monetary* – terms. This is obviously an important point and I will return to it.

## THE SPIRIT OF CAPITALISM

Of course, none of Protestantism's theological innovations were conceived primarily with practical economic activity in mind, but together they appear – accidentally and ironically – to have had a profound effect upon the emergence of the modern economic order. As the religious energy of the Reformation waned towards the end of the 17th century, the legacy of these theological innovations was such as to have enhanced the secular quality of modern life. As historian RH Tawney observed, for example:

> When the age of the Reformation begins, economics is still a branch of ethics, and ethics of theology; all human activities are treated as falling within a single scheme, whose character is determined by the spiritual destiny of mankind ... [but] by the Restoration the whole perspective, at least in England, had been revolutionized. Religion has been converted from the keystone which holds together the social edifice into one department within it, and the idea of a rule of right is replaced by economic expediency as the arbiter of policy and the criterion

of conduct. From a spiritual being, who, in order to survive, must devote a reasonable attention to economic interest, man seems sometimes to have become an economic animal, who will be prudent, nevertheless, if he takes due precautions to assure his spiritual well-being.[35]

The move from the traditional to the modern economic order may thus be said to have been a move from a world in which the chief concern was to protect the possibility of eternal blessedness *from* mundane economic activity to a world in which practical technological and economic endeavours were considered crucial to the pursuit of temporal and, by extension, eternal happiness.

However the origins of modern capitalism's unusual spirit are understood, and in spite of the fact that a number of other religious traditions have since proven able to emulate it, there is little doubt that free market capitalism continues to be animated by people who are pragmatic and activistic, who are largely liberated from traditional restraints with respect to economic activity, and who are open to new opportunities and ventures. These people are not undisciplined, however. Indeed, they are prepared to make considerable sacrifices and to delay gratification for significant periods of time in the interests of their ventures. They are people, Peter Berger observes in *The Capitalist Revolution,* 'marked by a high degree of rationality – not in the sense of philosophical or even scientific reason but by functional rationality, by a sober, no-nonsense, problem-solving attitude to life in general and, of course, to economic life in particular'.[36] 'Put differently,' Berger continues:

> what we have here is a 'calculating' individual – not, or not necessarily, in the sense that all human relations are perceived in terms of some sort of economic costs/benefits analysis (that is an anticapitalist stereotype) – but rather in the sense that specific sectors of life, and notably the sector of economic activity, are approached in a rationally calculating and planning manner. This individual is also animated by a strong

sense of ambition and the goals of this ambition are to be reached by means of competitive achievement. Finally, here is an individual who is open to innovation, as against one bound by the past. Indeed, there is a tendency within this individual to regard anything as better simply because it is new. This trait, of course, is highly relevant to the 'creative destruction' of capitalism.[37]

The experimental economy, in other words, initially required, and continues to require, ambitious and experimental individuals.

Still, it is important to stress that as crucial as the capitalist *spirit* was, it did not – and still does not – in and of itself produce the generalised prosperity that we are concerned to explain. Rather it needed – and still needs – to be empowered by institutional arrangements that bring buyers and sellers together, facilitate orderly and non-coercive exchanges between them, and enable buyers and sellers to learn economically relevant lessons from their exchanges. Here again, a good deal of scholarly effort has gone into trying to understand and trace the historical development of these arrangements. Rosenberg and Birdzell, as we have already mentioned, consider the plurality and flexibility of a number of western institutions – law, bills of exchange, insurance, rational taxation policies, etc. – to have been crucial to western economic development.[38] Yet in addition to institutions favourable to commerce, bourgeois entrepreneurs also needed to be empowered by methods that enabled them to allocate scarce economic resources in a rational – which is to say economically successful – fashion. Early capitalists, in other words, needed a way of determining whether their efforts were 'paying off' or not. Of course, anyone desiring to stay in business in today's world needs to do this as well.

'Rational', in this context, simply refers to the *relation*, or *ratio*, of means to ends. One is said to act rationally if one employs means appropriate to the realisation of ends that have been deemed in advance to be desirable. This sounds fairly straightforward and easy, but in practice it actually isn't. With respect to economic action, for example, not only do we have to contend with our own habits and passions but also with the weight of traditional taboos and practices that are very often irrational. We also need to have some way of *measuring* the effectiveness of the means we employ in relation to the ends we have chosen. In other words, both our purposes and our means of achieving these purposes must be made more or less visible, testable, and ideally *quantifiable* if we are to be certain that our actions are effective and hence rational.

Modern science is instructive in this connection. The scientific method relies on carefully controlled empirical investigation and places a strong emphasis upon explanation, repeatability and predictability, all in precisely quantifiable terms. For the scientist, the only relevant information is information that can, in effect, be 'seen' – which is to say 'objectified' in some fashion – and that can be abstracted into some kind of conceptual unity, quantified, measured and ultimately tested. As Lewis Mumford noted a number of years ago in his classic study *Technics and Civilization*, the method of the physical sciences rests fundamentally upon a few simple principles:

> First: the elimination of qualities, and the reduction of the complex to the simple by paying attention only to those aspects of events which could be weighed, measured, or counted, and to the particular kind of space-time sequence that could be controlled and repeated – or, as in astronomy, whose repetition could be predicted. Second: concentration upon the outer world, and the elimination or neutralization of the observer as respects the data with which he works. Third: isolation: limitation of the field: specialization of interest and subdivision of labor. In short, what the physical sciences call the world is not the total object of common human experience: it is just those aspects of this experience that lend themselves to accurate factual observation and to generalized statements. One may define a mechanical system as one in which any random sample of the whole will serve in place of the whole.[39]

Envisioning the world as a series of mechanical systems, Mumford continues, was a tremendously important victory for modern rational thought.[40] Not only did this victory enable us to *think* about nature in an entirely new way, but it enabled us to control natural processes much more effectively than ever before. Put slightly differently, we might say that the path toward modern technical-rational mastery of nature follows a simple conceptual sequence: *objectify, unitise* and *mathematise.*[41] It is on the basis of this sequence that prediction, planning and *rational* control of nature have become possible. Of course, as Mumford's comments indicate, this is not to say that modern science can 'see' everything. In fact, there are any number of things – freedom, spirit, will, love, etc. – that science per se cannot objectify. Yet the scientific method has proven remarkably effective in enabling us to take a measure of control over our material circumstances.

## THE MONEY METRIC

Our ability to take more effective control of our material circumstances *economically* closely parallels these developments in modern science and technology and is at least as significant. Indeed, as noted above, although the relatively high quality of modern living conditions is often attributed solely to modern scientific and technological development, it is doubtful that these developments would ever have touched the lives of ordinary people had they not been mediated, and in fact amplified, by the rationalisation of production, distribution and consumption. Here we may recall Rosenberg and Birdzell's observation that the experimental economy has proven to be an extraordinarily efficient link between science and the satisfaction of human wants.

How have we managed to link science and the satisfaction of human wants? In part, as we have already seen, by freeing entrepreneurs to take risks and to try new things, as well as by eliminating arbitrary and irrational influences upon economic life. Along this line, Rosenberg and Birdzell contend that a critical aspect of the West's growth system has been the absence of 'more than rudimentary political and religious restrictions' on innovation and commerce.[42] At an even more basic level, however, the rationalisation of modern economic life has, like science, depended upon a method of objectifying, processing, and analysing economically relevant information. Just as science developed procedures for objectifying, measuring and testing the natural world for the sake of taking control of natural processes, so modern economic agents have developed roughly similar procedures for taking control of economic processes. Instead of objectifying nature, however, economic procedures objectify and conceptually unify the world of *value*. It is the objectification of value that enables economic agents precisely to *test* the relationship between economic means and the end of economic growth.

Consider the importance of rational accounting in today's world, a matter to which we have recently become sensitive in the wake of the collapse of several large American corporations. Accounting makes it possible – or at least is supposed to make it possible – for entrepreneurs, managers and investors to precisely evaluate the relation of a variety of means and strategies to the end of profitability. It enables them to compare and assess the likely consequences of different courses of action, allocate resources effectively, plan and hopefully survive, which is to say to remain profitable in a competitive marketplace. Accounting techniques frame and edit information, simplifying the complexity of reality and absorbing uncertainty. The 'bottom line' that accountants produce for decision-makers does not reflect all possible interpretations and judgements but rather only those that are directly relevant to continued growth.[43] For want of such information, the modern business firm would fail in short order, which is precisely why the recent disclosure of deceptive accounting practices in large firms has so profoundly shaken our confidence in the market. It should come as no great surprise, then, to find that the likes of

Max Weber, Werner Sombart and Joseph Schumpeter have all emphasised the tremendous significance of rational accounting, and particularly of double-entry bookkeeping, to the development of modern capitalism.

Yet our analysis can be taken even further; for the instrument that enables accountants to reduce the complexity of economic reality in such a way as to absorb uncertainty, and the tool that enables us to represent this simplified reality in such a way as to facilitate decision-making and to 'give account' of the rationality of our decisions, is the simple abstraction that we call *money*. Money is the crucial instrument that enables us to objectify and conceptually unify the world of values. Money's conversion of reality into measurable, quantifiable units is what enables us to precisely assess, indeed to *calculate*, the relation between economic means and ends. It is the tool that makes *rational* economic calculation possible. Combined with institutional arrangements designed to facilitate peaceful exchange between rational buyers and sellers, money – or what economists typically call 'the price mechanism' – lies at the very heart of the market system. Prices in money indicate what the myriad of products and services are 'worth', both to those who produce them as well to those who consume them. Prices in money enable producers to determine what, when and for whom to produce, consumers to determine what, when and from whom they will purchase, and investors to determine where, when and with whom to invest. It is the price mechanism, in short, that efficiently links experimental technology with the satisfaction of human wants and it is one of the critical instruments of the modern age. As social theorist Georg Simmel noted so perceptively almost a century ago in his monumental study *The Philosophy of Money*, money both 'embodies and sublimates the practical relation of man to the objects of his will, his power and his impotence'.[44] Money has become, for many modern people, *the* absolute instrument.

But is this really new? After all, money has been around for a

very long time.[45] The answer to this question is both yes and no.
On the one hand, with respect to consumption, our interest in
money today probably isn't significantly different from that of our
pre-modern ancestors. People have always been concerned about
possessing money for the sake of all those things that money can
*buy*. Rather it is when we consider money's role in *production* that
we can begin to see a significant difference between the role that
money plays in modern, capitalist society and the role it played in
earlier, traditional settings. Along this line, we have already
referred to Schumpeter's comment that capitalism 'exalts the
monetary unit'. Yet capitalism does not exalt the monetary unit as
a unit of possession but rather as a unit of *account*, transforming
money – by way of double-entry bookkeeping and other accounting procedures – into an instrument of rational cost-profit analysis.[46] This is very significant because, as Schumpeter goes on to
stress, it is the cost-profit calculus and its precise numerical definition of economic inputs and outcomes that so powerfully pro-
pels the logic of modern enterprise.[47] The cost-profit calculus,
based as it is on money's numerical restatement of value, directs
producers to scale production up or down. It directs them towards
opportunities and away from failure, perhaps signalling the need
to produce something differently or to produce something altogether different. It is the 'monetisation' of value, in other words,
that enables producers to precisely adjust their resources and
means of production to the demand that actually exists for their
products.

And not only is the 'monetisation' of value crucial to decisions
related to present production, but in the context of economic
growth money also acquires a 'time value' as it is discovered that
through creative and intelligent use, money – as *capital* – can effectively reproduce itself as 'return on investment'.[48] Time, as the
archetypically bourgeois adage states, *is* money, and the growth of
capital over time is what accounts for the kind of expansion that
economists now measure and state in terms such as 'Gross

Domestic Product' and 'Gross National Product'. Such measures have become increasingly important – not simply to economists and policy-makers – but to the rest of us in capitalist societies as well. For we have all become increasingly aware that our plans for the future – from educating our children to retiring in comfort – will hinge to a large extent upon the rate of economic expansion. The role that money plays in modern capitalist society is not simply new but, as Simmel observed, has become 'absolute for the consciousness of value'[49] in a way that simply could not have been conceived by our traditional ancestors.

As money becomes absolute for the consciousness of value, it does not merely propel the logic of enterprise, but it also catalyses fundamentally new kinds of relationships between the individual members of bourgeois societies, further liberating them from traditional restraints. Money makes it possible for us to precisely 'contract' our relations to others and to be connected to them only insofar as we desire to be connected. It frees us from the plethora of restrictions and obligations that encumber relations and limit individual choice in more traditional settings.[50] As Peter Berger has noted:

> Capitalism liberates the individual by letting him step out of his particular frieze – provided, of course, he acquires the money to do so. Money, with its great power of abstraction, makes its possible to convert all socially relevant phenomena (goods, services, statuses, even identities) into units of specific monetary worth. The individual too can be so converted. The American phrase 'What is he worth?' illustrates this monetary conversion very graphically. Often this phrase has been cited as evidence of the 'dehumanizing' effects of capitalism. Maybe so, depending on one's ideal of 'humanity.' But the same phrase illustrates the liberating effects of capitalism. To assess a man's 'worth' in terms of the money he possesses ipso facto puts in brackets whatever 'worth' he may have by way of congenital and collective ascription: Nobody chooses his parents, but anyone, in principle, can accumulate capital.[51]

As Berger's comments indicate, money is far more than simply an economically useful instrument. Rather it has become, particularly within modern capitalist society, a critical criterion for social stratification as well as for determining social purposes. Indeed, given money's instrumental significance within the logic of enterprise, and given its revolutionary impact upon the sorts of relationships and self-understandings that give capitalist culture its distinctively bourgeois flavour, it would seem that money – what I have chosen to call the Money Metric – must lie very close to the essence of modern capitalism.

Turning our attention for a moment to the sorts of material and cultural influences we can expect capitalism to have on us and, indeed, upon anyone else who desires to get into the capitalist game, we might simply begin by noting that social theorists have, following the lead of Ferdinand Tönnies, commonly described the remarkable transition from a 'traditional' to a 'modern' social order in terms of a shift from 'community' (*Gemeinschaft*) to 'society' (*Gesellschaft*).[52] In a traditional 'community', what got done was determined and rather tightly circumscribed by kinship and tribal sentiments, habits, customs, and shared traditional meanings; now a great many of us live in 'societies' where what gets done is determined by individuals – including corporate 'individuals' – acting more or less freely and practically in the pursuit of their own (predominantly material) interests, limited only by a kind of liberal social consensus which sanctions private property and precludes overt coercion.

What is not as commonly noticed is how crucial the Money Metric has been within this remarkable transition. Yet as Robert Heilbroner comments at the beginning of his fascinating study of economic history, *The Worldly Philosophers*, after countless centuries we moderns have finally discovered a fundamentally new solution to the problem of survival beyond the ancient solutions of 'tradition' and 'command'.[53] We have invented a kind of game in which we assure our continued existence by allowing each other to do exactly as we each see fit, provided we follow a central guiding rule. The game, Heibroner suggests, is the market system, and the rule is simply that we must each do what is to our best *monetary* advantage.[54] The interplay of our actions against one another, as each of us does what is to our best monetary advantage, has resulted – astoundingly – not simply in the realisation of most (if not all) of the social tasks requisite for our continued survival, but also in the substantial improvement of our material standard of living. This, Heibroner writes, 'was the most important revolution, from the point of view of shaping modern society, that ever took place'.[55]

Heilbroner's judgement is surely correct. Indeed, the capitalist 'revolution' represents an *exponential* advance in our ability to take control of our material circumstances by means of the rationalisation of the production, distribution, and consumption of goods and services. As this rationalisation of economic action linked up with discoveries of modern science and with the techniques of modern technology beginning in the 17th century, it formed the immensely potent synthesis that we have come to call 'industrial capitalism', a system that has changed and continues to change our world in all sorts of far-reaching ways. Indeed, the impact of industrial capitalism has been nothing short of astonishing. It has precipitated a vast increase in human productivity and has ensured that scientific discovery and technological 'know how' have, for the most part, been geared towards improving the lives of ordinary people, empowering them and thus stimulating further discovery and innovation. Peter Berger states this succinctly in *The Capitalist Revolution*: 'Advanced industrial capitalism has generated, and continues to generate, the highest material standards of living for large masses of people in human history.'[56] No other economic system has come even close to matching modern capitalism's productive capacity.

As if generating high material standards of living were not enough, revolutionary capitalism has also given rise to a significant increase in personal freedom, opportunity and choice. This appears to be largely because bourgeois individuals have learned, by and large, to be rational and self-determining agents. They have become accustomed to pursuing freely their own economic interests and to taking advantage of opportunities. They have come to understand what it means to enter into contracts, conclude agreements, and establish and participate in voluntary associations of various kinds. It is not particularly surprising, then, that those who have become so accustomed to freedom in the economic arena have historically also been attracted to democratic institutions and chartered liberties. Along this line, prosperous entrepreneurs naturally prefer rational economic policies to irrational political intervention, and they typically come to believe that they ought to have a say in shaping policies that affect their enterprises. Successful capitalist enterprise, as we have seen, has always required a degree of immunity from irrational and arbitrary political interference, and the creative-destructive dynamic of the capitalist marketplace is such as to resist comprehensive political control in any event. For all these reasons Michael Novak asserts that '[p]olitical democracy is compatible in practice only with a market economy'.[57] Enterprising citizens, Novak contends, will inevitably insist upon political systems based upon suffrage, the separation of powers, and the declaration of individual human rights.[58] Peter Berger puts this same point more modestly after simply observing that all democracies are in fact capitalist, that no democracies are socialist, but that many capitalist societies are not (yet?) democracies. 'Capitalism', he writes, 'is a necessary but not sufficient condition for democracy.'[59] Berger goes on to posit that if capitalist development is successful in generating growth from which a significant proportion of a nation's population benefits, pressures towards democracy are very likely to appear,[60] and this would appear to be quite true.

Finally, as we have seen, the impact of revolutionary capitalism, and largely by way of its innovative use of money, has been such as to diminish the importance of traditional meanings and institutions. In the place of traditional communal reasoning, the rational cost-profit calculus has enabled us to project alternative futures, to conceive of novel ends, and to employ a variety of practical means to realise these ends. The modern system, as suggested in the Introduction, is one in which the past is all but replaced by the present and future, and innovation relentlessly trumps the status quo. I will have more to say about this in the next chapter, but this diminution of the traditional past does exact a price, and it is higher than we commonly realise. In the first instance, it creates a kind of cultural vacuum into which other newer and untried meanings must quickly flood – for example, that the matter of justice must now be resolved in largely *monetary* terms, or that many if not all of the social problems in capitalist society must now somehow dissolve under the application of enough money.

The evaporation of traditional meanings has also tended to make the possession of money important for *social* as well as economic reasons. Today if someone has enough money it doesn't really matter who they are, or even how they may have come by their money. Such people are deemed to be of social, and quite possibly of political, significance.

Interestingly, Tocqueville observed both of these tendencies during his visit to America at the beginning of the 19th century and I want to conclude this first chapter by briefly citing two of his observations.[61] On the one hand, Toqueville observed that an essentially bourgeois impatience with tradition had led the Americans to accept naively all sorts of rather radical modern methods. 'Of all countries in the world,' Tocqueville wrote, 'America is the one in which the precepts of Descartes are least studied and best followed.'[62] As a result of this, he commented:

> Most of the people in these [democratic] nations are extremely eager in the pursuit of immediate material pleasures and are always discontented with the position they occupy and always free to leave it. They think about nothing but ways of changing their lot and bettering it. For people in this frame of mind

every new way of getting wealth more quickly, every machine which lessens work, every means of diminishing the costs of production, every invention which makes pleasures easier or greater, seems the most magnificent accomplishment of the human mind.[63]

Tocqueville also noted that the American bias against tradition had the effect of making the simple possession of money far more important than it had been in an earlier, more genteel era. For when individuals are largely independent of each other, when they are no longer distinguished by birth, standing or profession, and when the prestige that once attached itself to tradition has vanished, there is hardly anything left *but* money to distinguish one individual from another. As a result of this, Tocqueville commented, 'One usually finds that the love of money is either the chief or a secondary motive at the bottom of everything the Americans do. This gives a family likeness to all their passions and soon makes them wearisome to contemplate.'[64]

Of course, in making these sorts of observations, Tocqueville was not concerned about defending the superiority of the *ancien regime* – far from it – but rather indicating several of the unintended consequences of liberal democracy's renunciation of traditional meanings and practices. For it was possible, he suggested, to become so entirely preoccupied with innovation, invention, and with the practical improvement of things that a people can forget where they have come from and, in effect, *who they are*. He wrote:

> The prospect really does frighten me that [the Americans] may finally become so engrossed in a cowardly love of immediate pleasures that their interest in their own future and in that of their descendants may vanish, and that they will prefer tamely to follow the course of their destiny rather than make a sudden energetic effort necessary to set things right.[65]

Tocqueville suspected that this loss of cultural vision was the unintended by-product of liberal democracy, and yet it occurs to me that it may also have been an unintended consequence of modern capitalism's 'exaltation of the monetary unit'. Indeed, if the love of money has become a chief or a secondary motive at the bottom of much that is done in today's world, this may have had less to do with greed – as, for example, traditional moral reasoning would suspect – than it has to do with the tendency of the Money Metric to empty the world of substance and meaning. Money, it seems, especially when it is placed at the centre of social life as it is in capitalist society today, tends to foster a peculiar *world view*. It becomes, in effect, a *metaphysic*. In the next chapter, I will explore a number of the implications of what Georg Simmel termed 'the *philosophy* of money', which may help us to see more clearly the nature of the dilemma that modern capitalism presents to us.

# 2

# UNINTENDED CONSEQUENCES OF CAPITALISM'S 'EXALTATION OF THE MONETARY UNIT'

> By being the equivalent to all the manifold things in one and the same way, money becomes the most frightful leveler. For money expresses all qualitative differences of things in terms of 'how much'? Money, with all its colorlessness and indifference, becomes the common denominator of all values; irreparably it hollows out the core of things, their individuality, their specific value, and their incomparability. All things float with equal specific gravity in the constantly moving stream of money. All things lie on the same level and differ from one another only in the size of the area which they cover.
>
> Georg Simmel, 'The Metropolis and Mental Life'[1]

I have suggested that the essence of capitalism consists in a disciplined, innovative and enterprising 'spirit' that has been empowered and indeed amplified by certain rational methods and tools. Such methods and tools have enabled entrepreneurs and managers carefully to adjust economic resources and the *means* of production to the *end* of profitability, and they function on the basis of the *objectification of value* made possible by the use of money. Linked with modern science's similar *objectification of nature*, capitalism's Money Metric, as I have termed it, has vastly increased human productivity, propelled the logic of enterprise and invention, and revolutionised the material standard of living in capitalist societies. Industrial capitalism has generated and continues to generate the highest material standards of living for large masses of people in human history.[2]

Modern capitalism has also given rise to significant increases in personal freedom in opportunity and in choice. Indeed, a relatively free market appears to be a necessary, though perhaps not sufficient, requirement of democracy under modern conditions.[3] 'Of all the systems of political economy which have shaped our history,' Michael Novak has observed, 'none has so revolutionized ordinary expectations of human life – lengthened the life span, made the elimination of poverty and famine thinkable, enlarged the range of human choice – as democratic capitalism.'[4]

It would be entirely appropriate, I think, for us to pause at this point in our analysis to consider just how fortunate we are to be the beneficiaries of such a system. Most of us would simply not be here were it not for the market economy's remarkable productivity, and the material quality of our lives going forward depends in very large part upon the system's continued generation of wealth. Small wonder, then, that many today would argue that the moral legitimacy of free market capitalism is established by its sheer facticity.

But just how far should we take this? Michael Novak, in the same work just cited, contends that democratic capitalism is simply the best system we can hope for this side of the kingdom of God. He believes that because the market system permits and indeed encourages individuals to take risks and to try new things in the pursuit of happiness so it unleashes powerful – and providentially ordained – forces for good in the world, though he admits that such forces are neither predictable nor explicable in terms of theory. At the conclusion of *The Spirit of Democratic Capitalism* Novak writes:

Almighty God did not make creation coercive, but designed it as an arena of liberty. Within that arena, God has called for individuals and peoples to live according to His law and inspiration. Democratic capitalism has been designed to permit them, sinners all, to follow this free pattern. It creates a noncoercive society as an arena of liberty, within which individuals and peoples are called to realize, through democratic methods, the vocations to which they believe they are called.[5]

Yet in spite of the fact that we ought to be grateful for capitalism's varied and sundry benefits, capitalist development has entailed certain costs that we would be remiss to ignore. I plan to discuss some of these costs in this second chapter. Of course, the costs most commonly discussed today are environmental. Many fear that industrial capitalism's continuing reliance upon oil and coal, and its tremendous generation of waste, not to mention the unintended consequences of its technologies and processes, are simply not sustainable in the long run. And I too find it difficult to see how industrial capitalism can continue to use and abuse nature without precipitating some kind of major ecological crisis – perhaps sooner rather than later. But the particular costs associated with capitalist development that I would like to discuss here are not environmental or material but rather *cultural, psychological,* and ultimately, *spiritual.* Such costs are perhaps best summarised under the heading of capitalism's *depletion of meaning.* As Peter Berger has commented:

> Modernization [with capitalism as a key component] operates like a gigantic steel hammer, smashing both traditional institutions and traditional structures of meaning. It deprives the individual of the security which, however harsh they may have been, traditional institutions provided for him. It also tends to deprive him of the cosmological security provided by traditional religious world views. To be sure, it gives him new opportunities of choice – that is, of freedom – but this freedom is purchased at a high price.[6]

Surely Berger is correct to point this out. There does seem to be an odd *emptiness* at the heart of capitalist culture, a kind of *weightlessness* that atomises and relativises all meanings and values.[7] The peculiarly ephemeral quality of capitalist culture is such as to leave us increasingly anxious, as comfortable as we may be otherwise. It is perhaps easy to exaggerate this. Francis Fukuyama, for example, lamented in a celebrated essay entitled 'The End of History' that the world has, in effect, reached the end of historical-political development because the liberal-democratic-consumer-capitalist system – or, as Fukuyama put it following Alexandre Kojeve, the 'universal homogeneous state' – has triumphed over its final remaining ideological challengers.[8] 'What we may be witnessing,' Fukuyama observed, 'is not just the end of the Cold War, or the passing of a particular period of postwar history, but the end of history as such; that is, the end point of mankind's ideological evolution and the universalization of Western liberal democracy as the final form of human government'.[9] Fukuyama went on to summarise the content of the universal homogenous state as liberal democracy in the political sphere combined with consumer capitalism in the economic.[10] Although both were originally western developments, the liberal-technocratic-consumer culture is, Fukuyama argued, destined to spread around the globe, alleviating poverty and eventually putting an end to ideological conflict. Fukuyama also hinted that the advent of the universal homogeneous state spells the end of religious striving and particularly of Christianity, for the modern system is founded upon the repudiation of Jesus' assertion that man does not live by bread alone. On the contrary, the moderns retort, man lives quite well by bread alone so long as he can be distracted – by means of entertainment and therapy – from asking imponderable religious questions. 'The end of history will be a very sad time,' Fukuyama commented toward the end of his essay. He continued:

> The struggle for recognition, the willingness to risk one's own life for a purely abstract goal, the worldwide ideological struggles

that call forth daring, courage, imagination, and idealism, will be replaced by economic calculation, the endless solving of technical problems, environmental concerns, and the satisfaction of sophisticated consumer demands. In the post-historical period there will be neither art nor philosophy, just the perpetual caretaking of the museum of human history.[11]

Perhaps it will only be the prospect of centuries of boredom, Fukuyama concludes, that will serve to get the historical process going again.[12]

Needless to say, Fukuyama's analysis is depressing and his thesis is debatable, but I believe he was correct to suggest that democratic capitalism does threaten our culture with spiritual vacuity, for the system does seem to discourage historical striving and/or religious questing. In the place of such self-transcending aspirations, the system offers us endless acquisition and consumption opportunities and holds out the promise of a perfectly comfortable and convenient lifestyle. The hegemony of the universal homogeneous state moved Heidegger to predict the onset of what he called 'the night of the world', in which all cultural development will be collapsed into technical uniformity and mindless consumption.[13] Weber described this outcome in terms of 'mechanized petrifaction embellished with a sort of convulsive self-importance', an endless era ruled only by 'specialists without spirit' and 'sensualists without heart'.[14] Nietzsche predicted the immanent arrival of 'the last men', who will think that they have invented happiness when in fact they have simply lost the capacity for self-transcendence.[15]

What can account for such despairing assessments of democratic capitalist culture? To begin to get a handle on this problem, we might simply recall Alexis de Tocqueville's concerns, cited at the end of the last chapter – that the citizens of democratic capitalism, having become so thoroughly preoccupied with material immediacy, seem content simply to 'follow the course of their destiny' rather than exerting the energy necessary, as he put it, 'to set things right'.[16] Tocqueville's concerns were restated earlier in the last century by Spanish philosopher José Ortega y Gasset in a study provocatively entitled *The Revolt of the Masses*. Ortega y Gasset contended that 'hyperdemocracy' and the fabulous expansion of modern consumer goods by means of modern industrial technology have together created a 'mass society' in which cultural and political aspirations have, in effect, been surrendered to the lowest common denominators of comfort, convenience and safety.[17] '[W]e live at a time,' Ortega y Gasset opined:

> when man believes himself fabulously capable of creation, but he does not know what to create. Lord of all things, he is not lord of himself. He feels lost amid his own abundance. With more means at its disposal, more knowledge, more technique than ever, it turns out that the world today goes the same way as the worst of worlds that have been; it simply drifts.[18]

My concern in this second chapter, then, is to try to determine just why it is that we seem to have become 'lost' in the midst of capitalism's abundance. Finding ourselves again, it seems to me, is a very important task today and will undoubtedly be necessary if we are to stand any chance at all of redressing capitalism's material and environmental problems. The specific thesis I will advance here is that our 'lostness,' for want of a better word, is in large part an unintended consequence of capitalism's Money Metric, that is, the system's 'exaltation of the monetary unit'.

Of course, it would be true to say that the 'anomic' quality of democratic-capitalist culture is, in one sense, simply the price we have *consciously agreed to pay* for freedom and prosperity, and that we should not be surprised by it. As we saw in the last chapter in connection with Rosenberg and Birdzell's analysis of the West's growth system, it has been the relative flexibility of western institutional life, as well the West's commitment to social and political pluralism, that has created – and still creates – the social 'space' within which entrepreneurial activity can flourish. And, as Michael Novak's comments have already indicated, the free market economy has always been very closely allied with a political tradition – often termed *classical liberalism* – in which it is asserted that the social good is best attained by affording individuals the greatest possible freedom of movement, even if this freedom is sometimes disorderly and disquieting. Novak, for example, believes that democratic capitalism not only permits us to experience alienation, anomie, loneliness and nothingness, but that it is actually renewed by these experiences, for they force us to reflect more deeply on the questions of meaning and purpose than we otherwise might.[19]

Now, whether any society is ever actually renewed by the experiences of alienation and anomie is debatable, but the movement from feudalism to capitalism has long been described in terms of the movement from a world in which individual well-being was believed to be the outcome of collective decision-making to one in which it is believed that social well-being is best served by allowing individuals to make as many decisions as possible for themselves.[20] Indeed, apologists for the market economy from Adam Smith's day to the present have made a point of stressing that the genius of the market mechanism lies precisely in the fact that it is able, by way of the 'invisible hand' of divine providence, to coordinate the purely self-interested actions of a mass of individuals so that they benefit society as a whole. As one observer has noted, summarising the gist of Smith's argument in *The Wealth of Nations*:

> The capitalistic project is not animated by a search for methods of institutionally liberating the inner drives of every man in the interest of the moral will. It is animated by a search for methods of institutionally liberating every man's natural instinct of self-preservation in the interest of external, politically intelligible freedom and peaceful prosperous life for mankind as a whole.[21]

Samuel Johnson's 18th-century quip summarises such observations nicely. 'There are few ways,' Mr Johnson wrote, 'in which a man can be more innocently employed than in getting money.'[22]

## THE PROFITS AND LOSSES
## OF CAPITALISM

Free market capitalism has never been envisaged as an 'ideal' system, nor does it require its participants to 'live well' in any kind of classical philosophical or teleological sense, nor even that they desire goodness per se. Rather it simply requires us to express our preferences rationally and in a relatively peaceful fashion. And not only does the capitalist project function 'in the interest of external, politically intelligible freedom', but, as Novak's comments earlier indicated, it has managed to produce real, which is to say humanly and socially intelligible, *progress* on this basis. It doesn't simply keep the peace, in other words, but it actually delivers some real social goods. This appears to be because the clash of interests and perspectives within capitalist society teaches bourgeois citizens tolerance and the art of compromise and often enables them to arrive at programmes and policies that, as Novak notes, 'strike closer to the good, the true, the real than any program simply imagined by one party alone, however noble or disinterested it may think itself'.[23]

The liberal caveat, of course, is that capitalist development will, at times, not appear to be very progressive, but will appear instead to be random, chaotic and anarchic. Intellectuals, we note, have tended to be particularly bothered by this. Yet classical liberalism begs us all to be patient with the market economy, to consider its past achievements, and to believe in the socially constructive potency of liberty. Socialism, after all, while undoubtedly more attractive intellectually, has never been made to work very well.

As an important aside here, we should note that the classical liberal commitment to individual liberty has not simply cleared the social 'space' for modern economic enterprise, but has also taken care to set up the rules of the economic game in such a way as to ensure that businesses are genuinely enterprising. To grasp the importance of this it may help to recall Weber's definition of capitalistic economic action as that 'which rests on the expectation of profit by the utilization of opportunities for exchange, that is, on (formally) peaceful chances for profit'.[24] The concept of 'profit', Weber insisted, and the conditions of exchange are *formally regulated* within the capitalist economy by accounting standards and laws that have, in turn, been shaped by theories about how markets should function as well as by liberal convictions about how best to achieve the common good. The liberal democratic polity, in other words, *requires* public economic activity to be practical, pragmatic, individualistic and geared towards profit and growth. Indeed, Weber believed that this classical liberal fusion of the formal, theoretical and ethical justification of the pursuit of profit had a great deal to do with capitalism's uniquely productive record.

This is why the burden of proof today still falls upon anyone who would suggest that there ought to be some other basis besides that of rational self-interest on which to make business decisions. After all, individuals and firms *must* pursue their own self-interest in a rational fashion for the market system to function efficiently and for the economy to continue to grow. The economy *must* continue to grow, furthermore, if it is to continue to attract the capital of rational and self-interested investors and if it is to support the material aspirations of all of those who participate in the larger system. Not only do the theory and formal requirements of enterprise today enjoin the practical pursuit of profit, but continued profitability is substantively sanctioned under the banners of 'growth' and 'progress'. To be in business within the market system today is, in effect, to be required to compete with others and to pursue perpetual growth by means of practical and rational production and consumption. That's just the name of the capitalist game.

Of course, liberal and, more recently, neo-liberal theorists have recognised the threat that individual liberty and laissez faire economic practices pose to moral order and social stability. But they have consistently suggested that the best way to buttress the social fabric is, again, to leave plenty of room in society for individuals to form associations with each other – clubs, service organisations, charitable foundations, churches – for the sake of upholding what these individuals perceive to be the good, the right and the true. Indeed, liberal theory has consistently stressed that democratic capitalism cannot thrive, and perhaps cannot even survive, apart from such associations. As American sociologist Robert Nisbet observed a number of years ago:

> Economic freedom cannot rest upon moral atomism or upon large-scale impersonalities. It never has. Economic freedom has prospered, and continues to prosper, only in areas and spheres where it has been joined to a flourishing associational life ... Capitalism has become weakest, as a system of allegiances and incentives, where these social resources have become weak and where no new forms of association and symbolism have arisen to replace the old.[25]

Speaking of 'replacing the old' here, it should be noted that even in spite of modern capitalism's 'creative destruction' of traditional institutions and meanings, the liberal commitment to individual freedom is such as to permit, and indeed encourage, anyone to try to recover what has been lost, so long as those who desire to make this recovery realise that their particular vision of the good, the right and the true cannot be imposed upon others. If the preservation of tradition is something you happen to value, Peter Berger observes at the conclusion of *The Capitalist Revolution*, then you would be well-advised to choose capitalism over socialism precisely because of this empirical linkage between capitalism and classical liberalism.[26]

Yet just because the liberal tradition *tolerates anomie*, envisages an associational strategy to cope with it, and perhaps even puts it to good use in certain respects, this still does not explain *why* capitalist culture seems so utterly prone to it. To get at the origins of the oddly weightless quality of capitalist culture, I think we need to look beyond the 'liberal compromise' to a number of the unintended side-effects of the operation of the market system itself.

Of these unintended side-effects, the most obvious simply have to do with *affluence*. Here we may recall John Wesley's classic lament over the impact of prosperity upon religious belief (c. 1740), cited by Weber in *The Protestant Ethic*:

> Wherever riches have increased the essence of religion has decreased in the same proportion. Therefore, I do not see how it is possible in the nature of things for any period of revival of religion to continue long. For religion must necessarily produce both industry and frugality, and these cannot but produce riches. But, as riches increase, so will pride, anger, and love of the world in all its branches.[27]

Although Wesley's comments suggest that this frustrating pattern is true of any period of religious revival, we note that modern industrial capitalism renders the relationship between industry and frugality and the production of 'riches' especially predictable. Within a democratic capitalist system, diligence and frugality will almost invariably result in upward social mobility and so also in the spiritual temptations that accompany such upward movement.

The atomisation and relativisation of meanings and values within capitalist culture is undoubtedly also due to the increasingly complex division of labour that rational economic exchange more or less naturally gives rise to as well as to the relentless social change that is all but guaranteed by the process of 'creative destruction'. In the context of the modern urban environment, and particularly when combined with rapid technological innovation, the operation of the market system poses a rather daunting challenge to anyone who would conserve *any* system of meaning, much less one inherited from the traditional past.

The market, furthermore, seems simply to be unable to 'see' certain kinds of substantive meanings and values. This was one of Alasdair MacIntyre's contentions in his influential book *After Virtue*.[28] Here MacIntyre distinguished between different kinds of 'goods' that it is possible to seek in economic activity. 'Internal goods', he suggests (following Aristotle) have to do with doing something well or achieving excellence in a teleological sense. 'External goods', on the other hand, do not relate to excellence or goodness *as such* but instead simply have to do with effectiveness in garnering external rewards such as money, power, prestige and status. External goods, MacIntyre continues, are typically the objects of competition out of which there must, by definition, be losers as well as winners. Internal goods, by contrast, may arise out of the desire to compete and excel, but when someone achieves an internal good it does not necessarily imply someone else's loss. On the contrary, internal goods benefit the entire community. This is because internal goods both require and sustain virtue.

The problem with the market system, MacIntyre felt, is that it is really only able to recognise and reward external goods. Indeed, he contended that the pursuit of excellence is actually redefined in capitalist society in terms of the external measures of efficiency and effectiveness:

> [I]n any society which recognized only external goods compet-itiveness would be the dominant and even exclusive feature ... We should therefore expect that, if in a particular society the pursuit of external goods were to become dominant, the con-cept of the virtues might suffer first attrition and then perhaps something near total effacement, although simulacra might abound.[29]

Of course, MacIntyre's indictment of the market system is not entirely fair and neither is it entirely accurate, for even if the sys-tem does not properly reward certain virtues – say, temperance – it does seem to reward others, such as honesty and transparency. And, as the recent collapse of several huge American corporations in the wake of the disclosure of apparently fraudulent accounting practices would seem to indicate, the system is relentless in its pun-ishment of certain kinds of vice.

Still, it does seem to be the case that the market system is geared more towards external rewards – efficiency, effectiveness, market share, etc. – than to the pursuit of goodness and excellence *as such*. Why is this? The answer to this question, I believe, has to do with capitalism's use of *money*. Indeed, the odd weightlessness of capitalist culture is – albeit perhaps unintentionally – a reflection of the objectification of value that is made possible by the system's 'exaltation of the monetary unit'.

Money, we have said, is a very powerful instrument. Indeed, it is one of the most powerful tools at work in our world today. And yet while tools empower us to do things, they also have a tendency to 'act back' upon us, often in unanticipated and unintended ways. This tendency is particularly interesting when it comes to the impact that tools often have upon our world view – that is, upon our conception of the nature of things and upon our understanding of the human task in the world. Although we commonly suppose that our tools are simply means to be put to use in the service of purposes that we have determined, our tools have an insidious way of altering these purposes and of modifying our determinations. 'To a man with a hammer,' Neil Postman has quipped along this line, 'everything looks like a nail.'[30] Paraphrasing Postman here, we might say that 'to a man with money, everything looks like a commodity – that is, like something that can either be bought or sold with money'. Along this line, I want to argue that our pervasive use of, and increasing reliance upon, the tool we call 'money' – the very tool that capitalism has put to such good use – has indeed subtly altered our interests and the things we think about. It has also subtly altered our symbols and the things we think with. Finally, it has subtly altered our communities and the forums in which our thoughts develop.[31] In short, the impact that money has had – and continues to have – upon modern capitalist society and culture has been *ecological*.

Karl Marx was among the first to recognise the conceptual – and *existential* – significance of money within the modern social system. Marx wrote:

> Since money does not disclose what has been transformed into it everything, whether a commodity or not, is convertible into gold. Everything becomes saleable and purchasable. Circulation is the great social retort into which everything is thrown and out of which everything is recovered as crystallized money. Not even the bones of the saints are able to withstand this alchemy; and still less able to withstand it are more delicate things, sacrosanct things which are outside the commercial traffic of men. Just as all qualitative differences between commodities are effaced in money, so money, a radical leveler, effaces all distinctions.[32]

While we are occasionally encouraged to reflect about the ethical implications of the ways that we spend money, the implications of assigning monetary values to things is not typically something that we worry very much about. We just do it. Indeed, it is difficult to imagine living in a modern society without routinely *having* to assign monetary values to things. Yet it is important to stress that everything – including even religious understanding – is indeed effaced in the alchemy of monetary commodification.

Beyond Marx, two other theorists who perceived the tremendous significance of money within the modern social system were Joseph Schumpeter, whom we have already had occasion to mention in connection with capitalism's 'exaltation of the monetary unit', and Georg Simmel, who authored the aforementioned study entitled *The Philosophy of Money*. The balance of this second chapter, then, will be devoted to considering first Schumpeter's and then Simmel's ideas about money, for both recognized a number of unintended psychological consequences of capitalism's Money Metric.

## SCHUMPETER'S 'CREATIVE DESTRUCTION'

Schumpeter is best known today for describing capitalism as a process of 'creative destruction', and we have already discussed him in connection with the role that money plays in capitalism's cost-profit calculus. But it is important to stress that Schumpeter was not actually very optimistic about capitalism's long-term prospects, in part because of the impact that money had upon the bourgeois imagination. The rational cost-profit calculus that capitalism had put to such good use, Schumpeter observed, actually rationalised more than business practices. Indeed, the logic of capitalism spilled out of the economic sphere and into art, philosophy and even religion. 'The capitalist process', Schumpeter noted, 'rationalizes behavior and ideas and by so doing chases from our minds, along with metaphysical belief, mystic and romantic ideas of all sorts. Thus it reshapes not only our methods of attaining our ends but also these ultimate ends themselves.'[33]

While capitalism's 'rationalization of the soul', as Schumpeter put it, does encourage prodigious technological development, and while it pushes political life in the direction of liberal values, it also 'rubs off all the glamour of super-empirical sanction' [34] and buttresses the plausibility of secularism, materialism, utilitarianism and, ultimately, nihilism. The capitalist process delivers certain material and political benefits, in other words, but at the cost of all meaning and belief that extends very far beyond creature comforts and strictly material progress. The system produces individuals who are largely free to construct their own meanings and purposes, but only within the confines of the here and now, and only by means of consuming the fruits of technological production. This trade-off, Schumpeter felt, was evident almost everywhere within bourgeois culture. In modern art, for example, he contended that capitalism's rationalisation of the soul interpreted the progression from the technical drawings of Leonardo da Vinci to Expressionism's 'liquidation of the object'.[35] The mundane and anti-heroic style of capitalist culture, Schumpeter wrote somewhat wickedly, 'could be easily – and perhaps most tellingly – described in terms of the genesis of the modern lounge suit'.[36]

More specifically, Schumpeter was concerned that by converting real property into shares of stock valued only in terms of price, modern capitalism had increasingly bled the life out of the *idea* of property.[37] This 'evaporation' of the substance of property, as Schumpeter put it, has subsequently had the unintended effect of disconnecting individuals from the material ground of political passion and moral order. It has affected the attitudes not only of those who own the stock but of *everyone* involved in the capitalist process. 'Dematerialized, defunctionized, and absentee ownership', Schumpeter commented, 'does not impress and call forth moral allegiance as the vital form of property did. Eventually, there will be nobody left who really cares to stand for it – nobody within and nobody without the precincts of the big concerns.'[38] The evaporation of real property combined with the anti-heroic and narrowly materialistic character of capitalist culture, as well as the hostility of intellectual elites, moved Schumpeter to answer the question, 'Can capitalism survive?' by saying, simply, 'No, I do not think it can.'[39]

Reflecting upon Schumpeter's analysis more recently in the context of corporate restructuring, leveraged buy-outs, and increasingly global securities markets, American sociologist Robert Nisbet observes that it isn't only the relationship to real property that evaporates within the capitalist process, but all sorts of other relationships evaporate as well. Indeed, the process creates a social atmosphere of increasing abstraction and irresponsibility.[40] 'Less and less seems to depend upon the traditional virtues of prudence and social responsibility in the husbanding of one's wealth,' Nisbet observes, 'and more and more depends upon Fortuna. Thus the atmosphere of the gambling casino begins to permeate not only one's economic but also one's familial and community life.'[41]

Everyone today wants to be rich, Nisbet laments, but at the same time no one wants to be too closely attached to property, family, church – in short – to anything that might limit their freedom to move in the pursuit of riches. Indeed, the mere possession of money seems to have become more important than the things money can buy and the relationships money was meant to serve.

Apparently the 'cash nexus' has developed a hold upon the modern imagination in ways that neither Marx nor the classical economists anticipated. Nisbet writes:

> If cash is the real thing instead of land development, factories, manufacturing, and the creation of products and services important to society, then certain other things will automatically assume importance too: frenzied buying and selling in the multitude of markets available in this country and throughout the world, a pronounced turning from product creation to simple ordinary money creation, and, as the record makes plain, leveraged buyouts, networks of mergers, takeovers, insider trading legal and illegal, poison pills, golden parachutes, and much else.[42]

Nisbet notes that the North American preoccupation with finance and 'money creation' began during World War I but accelerated rapidly following World War II. And it has only continued to accelerate since he published his observations in 1988. Indeed, crucial components of the 'globalisation system' discussed in the Introduction have to do in large part with the globalisation of new financial instruments and new techniques of money creation. Cash, for many people today, really does appear to be the only real thing.

## SIMMEL: MONEY'S ALCHEMY

Nisbet's comments about money's grip on the modern imagination provide a fitting introduction to Georg Simmel's neglected masterwork, *The Philosophy of Money*, first published in 1907. Although Weber's analysis of modern capitalism has attracted far more attention over the years, Simmel's analysis of the style of rationality fostered by the use of money, as well as of the ways that pecuniary calculation has captured the modern imagination, is every bit as insightful. Indeed, Simmel's analysis appears to have shaped Weber's own understanding of the process of rationalisation in a number of important respects.[43]

The key to money's distinctive 'alchemy', Simmel observed, is its objective worthlessness combined with simple arithmetic. After all, modern money is simply an abstraction, a symbol, a concept. It has no value in and of itself. Yet money is an abstraction that enables us to render all the multitude of things objectively and exactly. It renders all things 'visible' and measurable in terms of price. Money quickly and conveniently reduces all concrete and qualitative relationships to comparability, thereby making rational calculation and choice possible. Money is easy to use, and it is easy to learn how to use it. 'Money', Simmel observed, 'is the purest reification of means, a concrete instrument which is absolutely identical with its abstract concept; it is a pure instrument.'[44]

Although using money to 'objectify' things and relations in order to render them comparable in terms of prices for the sake of rational calculation might seem to be a simple and basically neutral activity, Simmel was concerned to show that in fact it is neither simple nor neutral. In the first instance, the use of money tends to reduce – in a way that, as we have seen, is closely analogous to the modern scientific method – all concrete qualities to mere *quantities*. It thus has the effect of flattening the world of things, stripping them of their colour, taste and texture. Because money performs this reduction so conveniently and reliably, it tends, ironically, to become *an end in and of itself.* 'Never has an object that owes its value exclusively to its quality as means ...,' Simmel wrote, 'so thoroughly and unreservedly developed into a psychological value absolute, into a completely engrossing final purpose governing our practical consciousness.'[45] He continued:

> This ultimate craving for money must increase to the extent that money takes on the quality of a pure means. For this implies that the range of objects made available to money grows continuously, that things submit more and more defenselessly to the power of money, that money itself becomes more and more lacking in quality yet thereby at the same time becomes powerful in relation to the quality of things ... The

inner polarity of the essence of money lies in its being the absolute means and thereby becoming psychologically the absolute purpose for most people.[46]

Of course as we have already noted, if modern individuals crave money, this is not simply due to greed, but to the fact that money has become more important *socially* as traditions and traditional social distinctions have disappeared. Yet money does not simply fill the void left behind by the passing of traditional society, rather it actively creates this void by liberating individuals *from* traditional bonds and, indeed, even from the bonds that extend from property and other objects of possession.[47] Money thus catalyses fundamentally new kinds of social relations within bourgeois society. It enables us precisely to 'contract' our relations to others and to be related to others only insofar as we *choose* to be related.

Yet Simmel observed that there is a dark side to this bourgeois liberation, for while we are increasingly dependent upon the *achievements* of others in these fundamentally new relationships, we are at the same time less dependent upon the personalities that lie behind these achievements.[48] Under modern conditions, in other words, a good deal of our interest in and involvement with others is purely *functional*. Our interest and involvement effectively end once the contracted services have been either rendered or received. And so while money does indeed liberate and individuate, it also depersonalises social relations. 'The more the unifying bond of social life takes on the character of an association for specific purposes,' Simmel commented in this vein, 'the more soulless it becomes. The complete heartlessness of money is reflected in our social culture, which is itself determined by money.'[49] Peter Berger summarises this point succinctly in *The Capitalist Revolution*:

> The world created by capitalism is indeed a 'cold' one. Liberating though it may be, it also involves the individual in countless relations with other people that are based on calculating rationality 'What is this person worth to me?', superficial

(the 'personalization' of salesmanship), and inevitably transient (the very dynamics of the market ensures this). Human relations too become subject to the 'creative destruction' of capitalism.[50]

Simmel went on to observe that the relatively impersonal quality of social relations based on the exchange of money for services – particularly when combined with money's ability to facilitate association for specific purposes – explains the increasing disparity between bourgeois culture's objective achievements, which are considerable, and bourgeois subjectivity, which tends to be rather impoverished. The money economy is remarkably productive and inventive, in other words, but it does not seem to foster the development of character, or at least not beyond fairly narrow limits. Simmel commented:

> If one compares our culture with that of a hundred years ago then one may surely say – subject to many individual exceptions – that the things that determine and surround our lives, such as tools, means of transport, the products of science, technology and art, are extremely refined. Yet individual culture ... has not progressed at all to the same extent; indeed, it has even frequently declined.[51]

Just imagine what Simmel would have to say about this discrepancy today – when we have completed mapping the millions of lines of code that make up the human genome, while at the same time we are aware that the average individual does not read even one book a year, and even then not much above the reading level of a 10-year-old.

Yet if bourgeois individuals are not encouraged to develop character per se, they are encouraged to become skilled and often very shrewd calculators. The money economy, Simmel observed, encourages us to transform the world into a series of arithmetic problems and to see the world through mathematical formulas. 'Only money economy', he commented, 'has filled the days of so many people with weighing, calculating, with numerical determinations, with a reduction of qualitative values to quantitative ones.'[52] However, as individuals have become more shrewdly calculating, Simmel observed, they have also become increasingly *cynical* and *blasé*.

The cynical individual, Simmel commented, simply comes to believe that everything and everybody is, in the end, purchasable with money. The cynic observes that even the finest and most excellent goods and experiences are more or less immediately available to anyone who has the money to buy them. Even more importantly, he notes that such goods and experiences are denied to even the most worthy of persons if they do not possess the necessary monetary means to acquire them.[53] Money seems to determine everything. Even things that appear at first glance to transcend the 'cash nexus' are always, in the end, revealed to be commodities of some kind, or at least so it seems to the modern cynic. 'The nurseries of cynicism', Simmel wrote:

> are therefore those places with huge turnovers, exemplified in stock exchange dealings, where money is available in huge quantities and changes owners easily. The more money becomes the sole centre of interest, the more one discovers that honour and conviction, talent and virtue, beauty and salvation of the soul, are exchanged against money and so the more a mocking and frivolous attitude will develop in relation to these higher values that are for sale for the same kind of value as groceries, and that also command a 'market price'.[54]

While those possessed by the spirit of cynicism are not particularly inclined to protest this state of affairs, and may even be tempted to derive pleasure from it, Simmel observed that others are tempted to cease feeling anything at all. Indeed, these others respond to the general reduction of quality to quantity, as well as to the increasing commodification of life, by simply becoming indifferent or, as Simmel put it, blasé. 'The essence of the blasé attitude', Simmel wrote:

consists in the blunting of discrimination. This does not mean that the objects are not perceived ... but rather that the meaning and differing values of things, and thereby the things themselves, are experienced as insubstantial. They appear to the blasé person in an evenly flat and grey tone; no one object deserves preference over any other.[55]

The blasé attitude, Simmel suggested, is a nearly perfect reflection of the completely internalised money economy.[56]

Interestingly, Simmel believed that the flat and grey quality of our experience of the world created by money accounted for the emergence of a kind of craving for excitement, for heightened stimulation and, as he put it, for 'extreme impressions' within bourgeois culture.[57] The satisfaction of such craving, he observed, can only be temporary within money culture, for the excitements, novel stimulations, and extreme impressions are quickly flattened by the same process that created our desire for them in the first place. Yet bourgeois individuals are all but compelled to seek excitement within money culture, and they are quite prepared to pay for it. 'The lack of something definite at the centre of the soul', Simmel wrote:

> impels us to search for momentary satisfaction in ever-new stimulations, sensations and external activities. Thus it is that we become entangled in the instability and helplessness that manifests itself [sic] as the tumult of the metropolis, as the mania for traveling, as the wild pursuit of competition and as the typically modern disloyalty with regard to taste, style, opinions and personal relationships.[58]

All these restless pursuits, Simmel felt, follow logically upon our intemperate reliance upon money today.

Of course, it did not take long for enterprising businessmen to recognise the opportunities that this bourgeois craving for heightened stimulation and extreme experience offered and continue to offer, making the contemporary market for entertainment enormous. Yet it is perhaps important to stress that while ventures like Disney World have only been developed over the last 50 years or so, the demand that has assured Disney's commercial success has been growing within capitalist culture for quite some time. As Christopher Dawson observed in the 1930s:

> We have entered on a new phase of culture – we may call it the Age of the Cinema – in which the most amazing perfection of scientific technique is being devoted to purely ephemeral objects, without any consideration of their ultimate justification. It seems as though a new society was arising which will acknowledge no hierarchy of values, no intellectual authority, and no social or religious tradition, but which will live for the moment in a chaos of pure sensation.[59]

It was Simmel's distinctive contribution to link the dawning of this new age with the peculiar operations of the money economy.

Clearly, Simmel anticipated a number of the more salient features of what has recently been termed the condition of *postmodernity*. As the specific contents of life have become more expressible in terms of money – which, recall, does not disclose what has been transformed into it – so the contents of life have become rearrangeable and reshuffleable. Life itself has come to be experienced as a kind of malleable mélange of commodified meanings, values and significations. In postmodern understanding, indeed, culture is a kind of game in which we simply rearrange meanings and values into new configurations, 'trying them on for size', as it were. All that may once have seemed so solid for us, as Marx and Engels put it so memorably, has increasingly 'melted into air'.[60]

And yet to the extent that we have been liberated from traditional constraints and meanings – indeed, from meaning *as such* – so we also find that we are increasingly at a loss as to what to do with our new-found freedom. For as money levels experience by making everything conveniently comparable in terms of simple arithmetical calculations, we begin to experience the world as a place devoid of *all* qualities and *all* purposes, as a place in which, as Simmel put it, 'all things lie on the same level and differ from one another only in the size of the area which they cover'.[61] Under such circumstances, Simmel observed, money – which is supposed to be simply a *means* to an end, simply a *tool* to be put to use in the service of our purposes – eclipses whatever purposes we may once have had and eventually displaces them in a kind of 'teleological dislocation'.[62] Money becomes *the only purpose*.

Simmel, of course, was not the first to notice money's teleological dislocation of human purposes within bourgeois culture. In the mid-19th century Søren Kierkegaard captured this with characteristic irony:

> In the end, therefore, money will be the one thing people will desire, which is moreover only representative, an abstraction. Nowadays a young man hardly envies anyone his gifts, his art, the love of a beautiful girl, or his fame; he only envies him his money. Give me money, he will say, and I am saved. ... He would die with nothing to reproach himself with, and under the impression that if only he had had the money he might really have lived and might even have achieved something great.[63]

Or, as Glenn Tinder commented similarly a number of years ago in *The Political Meaning of Christianity*:

> The subversion of physical reality reaches its logical climax when wealth is money. The amount that a person owns (his worth!) can be precisely calculated, thus giving to the independence and security wealth supposedly provides an appearance of unassailable objectivity. Holdings in money can be indefinitely increased; one's barns become infinitely capacious. And since money is readily convertible into a variety of physical possessions and personal services, it adds to the charm of ownership the allure of power. It is not surprising that 'the love of money' is characterized in the New Testament as 'the root of all evils'.[64]

Interestingly, particularly in light of Tinder's reference to the New Testament, Simmel observed that 'money culture' has managed to come to prominence historically only in situations where religious culture had, for whatever reason, already suffered a decline. 'There is no period of time in which individuals have not been greedy for money,' he wrote, 'yet one can certainly say that the greatest intensity and expansion of this desire occurred in those times in which the modest satisfaction of individual life-interests, such as the elevation of the religious absolute as the ultimate purpose of existence, had lost its power.'[65] As fundamentally religious beliefs and commitments ceased to define and shape modern purposes, it seems, money very quickly filled the void that religion had left behind.

In a similar vein, Simmel commented on the intriguing similarities between money as 'absolute means' and the traditionally religious conception of God as 'absolute agent'. There is little doubt, Simmel thought, that the feelings aroused in us by money are psychologically similar to those aroused in us by the notion of God. For money, too, 'rises ... above the whole broad diversity of objects; it becomes the centre in which the most opposed, the most estranged and the most distant things find their common denominator and come into contract with one another'.[66] It is no wonder, Simmel thought, that traditionally religious folk were so frequently suspicious of money. And it is no wonder today that in the absence of this traditional religious suspicion, money has so thoroughly captured the modern imagination.

This, I think, is as far as sociological analysis can take us. It reveals that in spite of the costly nature of environmental degradation and other problems associated with modern industrial development, other costs we have incurred for capitalism's remarkable productivity have been at the level of *meaning*. The nature of these costs are well-explicated by Simmel's analysis of the money economy and well-summarised under his heading of 'teleological dislocation'. Indeed, it is the dislocation of human purposes by monetary values that is perhaps the most serious of the unanticipated and largely unintended side-effects of capitalist rationality. It is this dislocation that interprets the odd emptiness that lurks at the heart of contemporary capitalist culture and it is this dislocation that seems to offer significant clues as to why we have become 'lost' amid our own abundance. The problem does not simply stem from the decadence that so often accompanies affluence, and it extends beyond the liberal tradition's refusal to commit itself to any one vision of social order. Rather the problem of capitalism's cultural 'weightlessness' stems from the Money Metric's relentless reduction of quality to quantity. This conversion, which modern capitalism puts to such good in the name of economic rationality and for the sake of economic growth, subtly, gradually, but seemingly inexorably, hollows out our entire world view, depriving us of any sense that life is inherently meaningful and that it has been endowed with qualities that far transcend monetary valuation.

So, is there anything we can do about this? Yes, I believe there is quite a lot we can do about it. Indeed, I believe that we *must* redress this problem before we stand any chance at all of successfully tackling many of the other issues associated with global capitalist development. But just as getting to the bottom of capitalism's peculiar weightlessness has required us to delve all the way down to the impact that money has had upon our most basic beliefs, so determining how to redress capitalism's cultural malaise will require us to revisit and perhaps rediscover a number of basic beliefs about the world, ourselves, and ultimately about God. We must move beyond strictly social-scientific analysis, and into *theology*.

# 3

# AN ECONOMY OF
# SHREWD STEWARDSHIP

I tell you, use worldly wealth to gain friends for yourselves, so that
when it is gone, you will be welcomed into eternal dwellings.
Luke 16:9 (NIV)

Clearly, we face a dilemma with respect to global capitalist development. On the one hand, democratic capitalism has been and
continues to be an astonishingly *good* system. No other political-
economic system in human history has been nearly as productive.
No other system has so emancipated so many *ordinary* people from
poverty, political repression, and the irrationalities and inefficien-
cies of traditional habits and customs. And yet we are aware that
this emancipation has also entailed considerable social upheaval
and that capitalism's social and material benefits have never been
evenly distributed. Moreover, in those societies where the market
system seems to have worked best, it seems to have advanced a
materialism, utilitarianism, and a kind of nihilism that has ener-
vated moral reasoning and thinned the culture of substance. The
resulting 'weightlessness' of capitalist culture, as I have termed it,

has rendered it all the more vulnerable to the market economy's 'creative destructive' process.

And so the question we face today, particularly since 1989 and the collapse of Eastern European socialism, is not whether industrial capitalism is preferable to socialism, for the economic superiority of the market system has become clear enough. Rather the question is, as Robert Bellah put it in 1991: 'Does the triumph of capitalism in our world today spell the rise of a kind of "market totalitarianism" that will eventually eat up the substance of society and culture?'[1] The answer to this question, I believe, is 'Yes, it almost certainly does.' Indeed, the Money Metric has eaten up quite a lot of the substance of our society and culture already, and it will only continue to do so if we do not somehow recover the wisdom to discipline its 'creative destruction' of meaning and purpose.

That modern capitalism presents us with such a dilemma should not surprise us. Just as the ground was 'cursed' on account of Adam's disobedience and so destined to yield thorns and thistles as well as sustenance, so we find that human systems such as free market capitalism always produce fruitless and poisonous side-effects, no matter how good and useful they may otherwise be. Liberal democracy presents us with similar ambiguities, and modern science and technology continue to be rife with all kinds of unintended consequences, many of them deeply perplexing. Along this line, Canadian political philosopher George Grant lamented that for all we have gained with our fabulous technological 'know how', we have also become increasingly aware that our capacity for appreciating the beauty and magnificence of the world has been diminished in the process of conquering nature. We long for the old 'gods' to manifest themselves again, but our anthropocentrism prevents it. Our technology has so thoroughly 'disenchanted' the world that, as he put it, '[t]here can be nothing immemorial for us except the environment as object'.[2] 'We live ...,' Grant wrote, 'in the most realised technological society which has yet been ... Yet the very substance of our existing, which has made us the leaders in technique, stands as a barrier to any thinking which might be able to comprehend technique from beyond its own dynamic.'[3]

Clearly, then, capitalism is not the only system in which unintended and undesirable costs have accrued along with varied and sundry benefits. Yet the fact that our constructions must nearly always produce unintended consequences, as well as the fact that some of these consequences will almost inevitably be injurious, does not mean that we should not try to overcome them. Indeed, from a Christian point of view, we *must* try to overcome them – or at least to temper them – for the sake of the love of God and the love of our neighbour. Christian social ethics, after all, is always a matter of trying to make the best of a bad situation. It is always a kind of salvage operation. Just how 'bad' the capitalist situation is may be debatable, and its relative goodness or badness is hard to assess, but there is no question that the free market economy presents us with a situation that begs to be made the best of. This is what I want to try to do – or at least to begin to do – in this third and final chapter. Granting capitalism's considerable economic and political accomplishments, I want to continue considering the Money Metric's seemingly inexorable erosion of traditional meanings and purposes for the sake of suggesting how we might go about arresting this erosion without necessarily having to abandon the system as such. Even more specifically I want to suggest how we might protect our *souls* from the anomie intrinsic to capitalism's 'creative destructive' process, as well as to suggest how we might best *use* this process to improve the quality of life for our neighbours as well as for ourselves.

I have said that a number of the market economy's more insidious side-effects have to do with the system's use of and reliance upon *money*. Of course, on the one hand, it is the pecuniary denomination of 'values' and the 'exaltation of the monetary unit' into a unit of account that has so empowered modern capitalism's inventive and entrepreneurial 'spirit' and enabled it to be so remarkably and consistently productive. But the system's 'rationalisation' of production, distribution and consumption has, as Schumpeter and others have noted, shown an insidious tendency to 'spill out' of the economic realm and into life in general – for example, into our understanding of nature, our conceptions of beauty and justice, our self-understanding, and even our spiritual ambitions. It is this 'spill over' that evokes the cynical notion – not uncommon in the West today – that everything and – even more distressingly – *everyone* is in the end sellable or purchasable. Indeed, this 'spill over' of economic rationality has tended to create a social climate in which the phrase, reputedly coined to describe Singaporean merchants – 'They know the price of everything, but the value of nothing' – would seem to describe a good deal of contemporary culture.

## THE SEARCH FOR MEANING

Paraphrasing Grant's comments about technology, the critical question we face in light of capitalism's 'exaltation of the monetary unit' is whether it is possible to comprehend the money economy from beyond its own dynamic. Put differently, can the Money Metric be fitted into some kind of larger perspective that would enable us to prevent genuinely human meanings and purposes from being flattened out by monetary valuation?

The answer to this question is 'Yes', though it may not be easy. Indeed, two types of suggestions have already been forwarded by Christian thinkers concerned about the erosion of meaning within capitalist culture. The first is the classically liberal suggestion that we must find meaning around the edges of the system by maintaining strong family ties and through our participation in voluntary associations and institutions – such as churches – that are dedicated to the preservation of traditional value systems. One of Berger's 50 propositions about prosperity, equality, and liberty in *The Capitalist Revolution*, for example, states: 'Capitalism requires institutions that balance the anonymous aspects of individual autonomy with communal solidarity. Among these institutions are, above all, the family and religion.'[4] Berger is surely correct to point this out, for capitalism requires a social atmosphere in which trust and transparency are taken seriously, and yet the system itself only has a limited capacity to generate such values. Instead, these and other values must, in effect, be imported into the economy from external moral sources, sources that would presumably provide discipline for the broader culture as well.

A second kind of suggestion stresses the importance of reinjecting normality more directly into the capitalist system. In an insightful study entitled *Capitalism and Progress: a diagnosis of western society,* Dutch economist Robert Goudzwaard argued that much of what ought to constitute the richness of human existence has in the modern situation been eclipsed by the twin objectives of economic growth and technological advancement.[5] This 'idolisation' of progress, as Goudzwaard termed it, has resulted in 'a persistent narrowing of human relations and purposes to technical and economic achievements as ends in themselves',[6] a problem implicit in virtually all modern ideologies, for example liberalism, socialism and Marxism, as well as nationalism in its many varieties. All these ideologies have been geared largely towards legitimating material progress, thereby emphasizing only limited aspects of human existence to the exclusion of many others. What desperately needs to be done, Goudzwaard concluded, is to reassert the full range of human meanings and purposes and to liberate them from their subjection to economic growth and 'progress'.

Both sorts of suggestions are very good. Still, I have come to wonder whether both are not crippled at the very outset by the 'alchemy' of monetary valuation. After all, isn't one of the more perplexing problems we face that our understanding of 'value' has itself been substantially *de*valued? Haven't our families, our associations, even our churches suffered under the commodification of meaning and purpose? Furthermore, to suggest that we must somehow reinject Christian values into the capitalist system, quite apart from the political difficulties associated with doing so under the banner of religion today, would seem to assume that we are capable of choosing and, in effect, 'denominating' values differently. But isn't this precisely the problem, that we have under capitalism's mentorship come to believe that meanings and values are things that *we* choose, perhaps believing even that they are things that *we* construct?

Admittedly, associational life within capitalist society continues to thrive, and it continues to be crucial to the system as well as to the culture at large, and the last thing Goudzwaard would want to advocate is the imposition of Christian values upon a culture loath to accept them. Still, it seems to me that if we are to comprehend the money economy from beyond its own dynamic, we must do two additional things. The first, which we have already done, is to examine capitalism's use of money and the social-psychological toll that the cost-profit calculus has taken upon our self-understanding. The second task must be to probe the contours of the modern intellectual 'climate of opinion', which, as Simmel observed, offered so little resistance to the substitution of 'the absolute instrument' for divine agency at the centre of things. What, in short, are the deepest presuppositions embedded within our money economy? Perhaps if we can tease these out we can begin to determine the best way to arrest the Money Metric's erosion of meaning and purpose.

## A LEVELLING OF VALUES

At one level the bourgeois world view is simply practical and pragmatic. It is interested in 'getting things done' or, as Tocqueville observed, in improving the material conditions of life by way of inventing new devices, increasing productivity, diminishing the costs of production, hastening transport, facilitating communications, opening up new markets for distribution, and so forth. From the purely practical point of view, these sorts of endeavours would seem to encompass most human purposes. Indeed, recall that Tocqueville noted that their success in the realm of the practical had encouraged early 19th-century Americans to imagine that everything in the world must somehow be explicable in technical terms. 'Hence,' Tocqueville observed, 'they have little faith in anything extraordinary and an almost invincible distaste for the supernatural.'[7]

Yet it would be a mistake to imagine that the narrow preoccupation with the practical is simply an American problem. In a celebrated analysis of the Enlightenment, historian Carl Becker observed that since the 18th century the entire modern intellectual 'climate of opinion', as he put it, has been very largely practical and pragmatic. The atmosphere that sustains modern thought, Becker observed:

> is so saturated with the actual that we can easily do with a minimum of the theoretical [by which he means speculative and/or metaphysical]. We necessarily look at our world from the point of view of history and from the point of view of science. Viewed historically, it appears to be something in the making, something which can at best be only tentatively understood since it is not yet finished. Viewed scientifically, it appears as something to be accepted, something to be manipulated and mastered, something to adjust ourselves to with the least possible stress.[8]

So long as we can make efficient *use* of things, Becker argued, we don't feel any great need to understand them. '[I]t is for this reason chiefly,' he noted, 'that the modern mind can be so wonderfully at ease in a mysterious universe.'[9]

Yet there is also an ideological *edge* to the apparently innocent practicality of the modern mind. It is not simply interested in the practical improvement of things. Rather it is also decidedly *dis*interested in beliefs and value systems that would seem to place apparently irrational and dogmatic restrictions upon the programme of practical improvement. Steven Seidman, for example, has suggested that modern thought has, at least since the Enlightenment, consciously *precluded* belief in what he terms 'cosmic order', with its presuppositions of external fixity, finiteness, hierarchy and teleology.[10] In place of such older and largely religious beliefs, modern thought has substituted an entirely 'secular order' that is infinite, changing, governed only by efficient and non-teleological causality, and in which all entities are believed to lie on the same level of being. This secular order, so modern thinkers have believed, allows much more room for human freedom and creativity, and it cannot so easily become the object of religious conflict. 'Translated into sociocultural terms', Seidman noted, 'secularism reveals a pronounced drift toward liberal values and orientations: progress, tolerance, egalitarianism, and empiricism.'[11]

It is not difficult to spot the affinity between such radical egalitarianism and the radical levelling effect of the use of money. Just as the use of money encourages us to 'objectify' the world of things, to lay them all out on the same plane of being, and to assign values *to* them, so the modern secular order is decidedly *anthropocentric*. There is no inbuilt hierarchy of values, so the typically modern argument runs, rather we must be left entirely free to value or not value things according to purposes that we have set for ourselves. Within this secular order, then, the human task in the world is understood to be that of 'knowing for the sake of making', and the principal virtue is that of *control*. Indeed, within this new secular order life is conceived as a 'struggle for existence' in which our survival is believed to depend upon our skill at becoming, as Descartes put it so memorably, 'the masters and possessors of nature'.

Of course, on the one hand this modern emphasis upon taking control of things is largely innocent and geared only to making incremental improvements to our material standard of living. It is just this kind of 'control' that democratic capitalism seems to facilitate so marvellously. Michael Novak observes, for example, that:

> Capitalism is very much (as the word suggests) a system of the head. Practical intelligence orders it in every detail. It promotes

invention and fresh ideas. it strives constantly for better forms of organization, more efficient production, and greater satisfaction. It plans for the long run as well as the short. It orders materials, machines, producers, salesmen, and consumers. It organizes means and ends. It constantly studies itself for improvement.[12]

Yet the modern preoccupation with control seems to many observers to extend far beyond the simple desire to improve things and, indeed, to amount to a kind of *obsession*. Commenting 70 years ago with respect to industrial development in Europe, Romano Guardini wrote:

> A century-long search for knowledge of nature has achieved a certain measure of insight into its laws. But that has made it possible to break into the closed nexus of nature. Individual forces such as steam, electricity, and chemical energy have been taken out of their natural context. We know their rational laws, and on the basis of this knowledge we can unleash their power. Something in us corresponding to this rationally unleashed energy – a specific attitude, craving, approach, a desire for mechanical and rational works – has arisen and placed these forces at our disposal, creating for them the intellectual plane on which we can see and exploit them with increasing fullness.[13]

It is not difficult to imagine that such a specific attitude would have been quick to grasp the practical implications of money's objectification of the world of 'value' for the sake of rational calculation and control.

The archetypically modern desire to take control of things has required modern thought to significantly narrow its field of vision, however. Instead of contemplating the vast array of things and beholding their mysterious qualities, the modern emphasis has, for the most part, been focused on concepts and the construction of theories, methods and techniques – in short – on a variety of strategies that promise to yield the fruit of practical mastery. As we have seen already in connection with modern science, such strategies work on the basis of their ability to objectify and conceptually unify the world of things. For once things have been rendered objectively 'visible' to theory, and once they have been pressed into some kind of conceptual scheme, they can be quantified, measured, tested and, ultimately, put to use.[14] It is this persistent narrowing of our field of vision for the sake of taking control of things that accounts for what has been described as modernity's 'disenchantment' of the world. Weber considered this 'disenchantment' to be of singular importance for modern development. It has meant that there can be no recognition of mysterious or incalculable forces in the world, and it has led to the belief that we ought, in principle, to be able to 'master all things by calculation'.[15]

And so modern thinkers have – occasionally consciously and explicitly, but often only unconsciously and implicitly – set about disclaiming traditional wisdom and traditionally religious interpretations of the world. Along this line, recall Tocqueville's intriguing observation that, while few early 19th-century Americans had probably ever read Descartes – indeed, most had probably never even heard of him – nevertheless American society corresponded quite closely to Cartesian principles. It was largely sceptical, individualistic, pragmatic, activistic and secular in outlook.

It is easy to poke fun at the narrowly practical quality of bourgeois culture, just as it is easy to exaggerate the nihilistic tendencies implicit within modern secular humanism. Yet the point of the foregoing analysis has been to do neither but rather simply to notice that, given the practical bent of the modern mind, it is not particularly surprising that we have not been concerned about offering more resistance either to the pecuniary reduction of quality to quantity or to the market economy's 'creative destruction' of culture. It is also not particularly surprising that practical technological and economic 'progress' has become, in effect, an end in itself in capitalist society. After all, our discussion of the modern secular order has disclosed a world view in which human existence is very largely conceived in terms of making the future by means of technological and economic mastery. It is a world view in which thinking can only, by and large, be conceived in terms of calculation and planning. All of this, as Grant saw so clearly with respect to modern technology, effectively stands as a barrier to any thinking that might comprehend the Money Metric from beyond its own dynamic.

What has been lost to us, Grant believed, is a way of understanding the world and ourselves that doesn't flatten everything – and indeed *everyone* – onto a kind of level objective plane. What has been lost to us, he wrote:

> [is] the recognition that our response to the whole should not most deeply be that of doing, nor even that of terror and anguish, but that of wondering or marveling at what is, being amazed or astonished by it, or perhaps best, in a discarded English usage, admiring it; and that such a stance, as beyond all bargains and conveniences, is the only source from which purposes may be manifest to us form our necessary calculating.[16]

The solution to our problem, in other words, does not so much lie in the reassertion of different values as it does in *the recovery of a way of seeing the world that would enable us to begin again to apprehend its value.*

## RECOVERING GRACE

Grant's comments echo those expressed by Jewish philosopher Martin Buber in his classic *I and Thou*.[17] To the extent that we desire to achieve control over the world, Buber suggested, we will of course be attracted to the utility of rendering it 'objectively', for rendering the world in terms of potentially manipulable objects is far more conducive to effective management than contemplating the world, admiring it, entering into genuine dialogue with it, and caring for it. But Buber observed that there is a high price to be paid for the convenience of objectification. 'The unbelieving marrow of the capricious man', he wrote, 'cannot perceive anything but unbelief and caprice, positing ends and devising means. His world is devoid of sacrifice and grace, encounter and presence, but shot through with ends and means.'[18] The world of 'capricious man', in other words, is lifeless. It is full of moving objects but largely shorn of persons. To the extent that we accommodate ourselves to this world of objects, furthermore, so we will eventually become 'objects' even to ourselves.

Buber's provocative suggestion that the modern world is devoid of *grace* is one that I would like to pursue below – and not simply because I think his description is accurate but, more importantly, because I believe that it will only be as we recover the capacity to apprehend and experience grace that we will be able to redress the sorts of problems that we have been discussing. Put somewhat differently, it will only be as we begin again to see that our life and work in this world are ultimately the *gifts of God* that we will be able to prevent the Money Metric from eating up the substance of our culture.

Pursuing Buber's suggestion that the 'capricious man' cannot perceive anything beyond positing ends and devising means, I want to discuss another classic, *The Everlasting Man*, which was written by GK Chesterton at about the same time that Buber penned *I and Thou*. One of the many things that Chesterton set out to do in *The Everlasting Man* was to defend the marvellously gracious quality of the Christian religion over and against a number of other far less gracious, yet nevertheless perennially attractive, religious options. One of these, Chesterton believed, is the 'religion' that seems always to lurk beneath the surface of commercial civilisations – the 'religion' of practicality, control, and 'getting things done'. Yet it is also, as Chesterton saw very clearly, a religion of cruelty and, above all, of *fear*.

In a chapter entitled 'The War of the Gods and Demons', Chesterton briefly recounts the Punic Wars that pitted the Romans against the North African city of Carthage during the 3rd century BC. The Carthaginians were sophisticated and wealthy, technologically advanced, supremely practical, and clever. Yet Chesterton observes that their practicality was born ultimately of a very deep-seated pessimism. There is 'a tendency in those hungry for practical results', he observed, 'to call upon spirits of terror and compulsion ... There is always a sort of dim idea that these darker powers will really do things, with no nonsense about it.'[19] Why, Chesterton queries his readers, does it so often seem to be the case that 'men entertain this queer idea that what is sordid must always overthrow what is magnanimous ...?'[20] They do so, he went on to reply:

> because they are, like all men, primarily inspired by religion. For them, as for all men, the first fact is their notion of the nature of things; their idea about what world they are living in. And it is their faith that the only ultimate thing is fear and therefore that the very heart of the world is evil. They believe that death is stronger than life, and therefore dead things must be stronger than living things; whether those dead things are gold and iron and machinery or rocks and rivers and forces of nature.[21]

Sadly, the specific religion that appears to have inspired the Carthaginians involved the worship of the cruel and terrible god Moloch and required them periodically to throw hundreds of their infant children into a large furnace.

Chesterton believed that God saved the ancient world from the brutality of the Carthaginian religious vision by eventually allowing the Romans to prevail in the Punic Wars, but he observed that the religious vision of the Carthaginians has continued to attract those anxious to 'get things done' in this world. Indeed, it has continued to pose a profound threat to any religious vision – and particularly the Christian one – that would affirm that life must ultimately prevail over death. 'It may seem fanciful', Chesterton wrote, 'to say that the men we meet at tea parties or talk to in garden parties are secretly worshippers of Baal or Moloch. But this sort of commercial mind has its own cosmic vision and it is the vision of Carthage.'[22]

Needless to say, Chesterton's comments are troubling and contentious, particularly his suggestion that ordinary businesspeople are secretly the worshippers of Moloch. And yet we note that the fear that, as Chesterton put it, 'the very heart of the world is evil' is actually a very common fear, even if it isn't commonly discussed. Most often it is hidden behind our anxiety in relation to *fate*. As Glenn Tinder stressed in a provocative study entitled *Against Fate: an essay on personal dignity*:

> Fate is all that threatens and befalls us. It comes upon us from without, often strange and uninvited, always at enmity with personal being. In words made commonplace by our familiarity with fate, it is 'meaningless' or 'absurd.' Fate may be fragmented and appear in the form of disjointed circumstances, or it may be massive and unified, even predictable. It may be experienced in recurrent jolts or in situations that devour us. It is always alien and dangerous. [23]

The fear of fate, Tinder continued, has loomed particularly large in the modern imagination. Indeed, the entire modern project has, in effect, been premised upon the assumption that fate must somehow be mastered if we are to survive in the world. One of the early and more significant architects of modernity, Niccolo Machiavelli, emphasised the crucial importance of mastering 'Fortuna', or fate, by any means necessary.[24] Whereas earlier political philosophy assumed that the natural order of things was deeply good and that it would sustain our lives if we could learn (by way of cultivating the virtues) how to live rightly within it, Machiavelli contended that the world was something that had to be made to serve human interests. Recall also Descartes' contention, mentioned above, that the genius of the scientific method was such that it might finally render us 'the masters and possessors of nature'. Only by taking control of nature, Descartes stressed, can we ensure our comfort and security. If such control requires us to 'objectify' the world of things, other people, and perhaps even our-selves, and if it requires us to reduce all qualities to mere quanti-ties for the sake of rational calculation, this is simply the price we have to pay for survival in the midst of an indifferent and fateful universe – or so the modern argument runs. For lurking beneath the surface of modern confidence is the fearful suspicion that the world is indifferent – and perhaps inimical – to human happiness, that it only reluctantly and grudgingly permits us to carve out space for our lives, and that such space can only be constructed more or less violently by means of 'dead' forces such as machinery and money.

Given modernity's deep-seated fearfulness, then, particularly in light of Chesterton's comments about the deeply pessimistic religiosity that so often animates commercial civilisation, we begin to suspect that our use of money today extends far beyond simple convenience, even beyond money's utility within rational economic calculation. Indeed as Simmel noted – though he declined to discuss it – there is a *spirituality* implicit in modernity's preoccupation with money. Money, so it is tacitly believed, is ultimately the only thing that one can really rely on. It provides the only final security. Jacques Ellul made this point a number of years ago in a provocative study entitled *Money and Power*. Ellul wrote:

> Nothing, whether in human nature or in the nature of things, whether in technology or in reason, adequately explains the original act of creating and accepting money. Nothing explains the blind confidence that we continue, in spite of all crises, to place in money. This is an absurdity which neither economists nor sociologists are able to clarify.[25]

The absurdity of money, Ellul continued, is only finally explicable in terms of spirituality, in terms of idolatrous worship. 'If people everywhere place such importance on the symbol of money,' he observed, 'it is because they have already been seduced and inter-nally possessed by the spirit of money.'[26]

Ellul's comments, of course, recall Jesus' reference to 'mammon' in the Gospel of Matthew, which I will cite at length:

> Do not lay up for yourselves treasures on earth, where moth and rust consume, and where thieves break in and steal, but lay up for yourselves treasure in heaven, where neither moth nor rust consumes and where thieves do not break in and steal. For where your treasure is, there will your heart be also. The eye is the lamp of the body. So if your eye is sound, your whole body will be full of light; but if your eye is not sound, your whole body will be full of darkness. If then the light in you is darkness, how great is the darkness! No one can serve two masters; for either he will hate the one and love the other, or he will be devoted to the one and despise the other. You cannot serve both God and mammon. Therefore I tell you, do not be anxious about your life, what you shall eat, what you shall drink; nor about your body, what you shall put on. Is not life more than food, and the body more than clothing? Look at the birds of the air: they neither sow nor reap nor gather into barns, and yet your heavenly Father feeds them. Are you not of much more value than they? And which of you by being anxious can add one cubit to his span of life? And why are you anxious about clothing? Consider the lilies of the field, how they grow; they neither toil nor spin; yet I tell you, even Solomon in all his glory was not arrayed like one of these. But if God so clothes the grass of the field, which today is alive and tomorrow is thrown into the oven, will he not much more clothe you, O men of little faith? Therefore do not be anxious, saying, 'What shall we eat?' or 'What shall we drink?' or 'What shall we wear?' For the gentiles seek all these things; and your heavenly Father knows that you need them all. But seek first his kingdom and his righteousness, and all these things shall be yours as well. Therefore do not be anxious about tomorrow, for tomorrow will anxious for itself. Let the day's own trouble be sufficient for the day. (Matthew 6:19-34, RSV)

There are many things that we would need to say if we were to properly exegete this remarkable passage, but there are several points we can mention briefly in light of our discussion. The first is that Jesus describes 'mammon' not simply as a possible object of worship but also as a kind of 'master' to whom service *must* be rendered if it is worshipped. The second is that Jesus suggests that we are moved to worship mammon primarily out of anxiety and fear of not having our basic material needs met. And the third is that our anxiety and fear disclose a fundamental – and to Jesus' mind almost ridiculous – lack of trust in the goodness of God.

The Christian religion teaches that anxiety, fear and mistrust have entered the world through *sin*, which is to say, through the prideful desire to be gods unto ourselves or, as the evil serpent in Genesis puts it, '*as God*, knowing good and evil'. From a Christian point of view, we expect to find pride and the desire for autonomy very closely bound together with fear and mistrust, and we expect all of them to be bound together in a kind of anxious search for security *apart from*, and all too often *over and against*, the living God. This, according to Christian teaching, is the way of our fallen world.

Surrendering to anxiety and fear and choosing to serve mammon, while perhaps resulting in a measure of material security, further blinds us to the goodness of God, rendering us all the more incapable of placing faith in him. This is why we cannot serve both God and mammon, for trusting in the latter blinds us even to the possibility of trusting God. Service to money insidiously empties the world of grace, leaving it full, as Buber put it so memorably, of 'unbelief and caprice, positing ends and devising means'. It declines our hearts into cynicism and indifference.

'When we claim to use money,' Ellul commented, 'we make a gross error. We can, if we must, use money, but it is really money that uses us and makes us servants by bringing us under its law and subordinating us to its aims.'[27] In light of our previous discussion of the unintended consequences of modern capitalism's 'exaltation of the monetary unit', it is clear that Ellul is quite right about this. Money has become much more than simply a tool within bourgeois culture. Rather it has become a kind of end in itself and indeed the final purpose for a great many people. It has essentially become a 'god' to whom service must be rendered and for the sake of which all sorts of sacrifices must be made.

But assuming that we do not want to serve mammon, what would our refusal to serve money look like? Most of us, I think, know intuitively what it would look like, at least negatively: we would not be gluttonous and miserly and materialistic and so forth. For the most part, Christian moral instruction pertaining to money and possessions has stressed just these sorts of moral failings. But how can the refusal to serve money be construed more positively? After all, the ethic informing our use of money and possessions cannot simply be framed in the negative. Along this line, and for lack of a better word, I think the hallmark of such a positive ethic ought simply to be 'lightheartedness'. This point was brought home for me a number of years ago by Richard John Neuhaus in a short article intriguingly titled 'Wealth and Whimsy'.[28] Neuhaus wrote:

> The point is that wealth – having it or producing it – really does not matter that much. This point is missed both by the avaricious, who become captive to their possessions, and by religiously driven ideologues promoting designs for a just economic order. Both are in danger of attributing an ultimacy to something that is, at best, pre-penultimate. Both take wealth altogether too seriously. A theologically informed appreciation of economic life and the production of wealth should be marked by a sense of whimsy and wonder in the face of the fortuitous, contingent, chancy, and unpredictable realities of economic behavior.[29]

I believe Neuhaus is largely but not entirely correct about this, for our 'lightheartedness' should stem not simply from admiration for all the things free economic agents are able to create but also from – indeed primarily from – our *trust in God*. A theologically informed appreciation of economic life, in short, must be marked by a decided lack of anxiety. For rendering service to God over and against 'mammon' is, by and large, *to trust him, to believe that he cares for us, and to rest in his promises to provide for our needs.*

Spelling this out in terms of our analysis, we might say that over and against the fearful modern suspicion that the universe is cold and indifferent and possibly even inimical to our best interests, we should, as Christians, affirm the gracious goodness of the living God as well as the deep goodness and giftedness of being. This is perhaps the most basic witness we can have within a culture that, as we have seen, has been moved to rely upon the alchemy of monetary commodification out of the deep fear that the world must somehow be mastered and possessed if we are to survive within it. Indeed, the single most subversive and ultimately redemptive idea that we can set loose within the capitalist world today is the simple recognition that *life is a gift.*

The implications of this idea are several. In the first instance, it means that we have not simply been 'thrown' into existence and that our survival does not depend simply upon our cunning and ingenuity. Rather we have been brought forth into a world that is *alive* with purposes that, far from being inimical to our best interests, have been ordered in such a way as to sustain our lives and render them fruitful. 'Look at the birds of the air,' Jesus implores us, 'they neither sow nor reap nor gather into barns, and yet your heavenly Father feeds them. Are you not of much more value than they?'

As an aside, we note that the repetitive properties of natural order have tempted modern thinkers to assume that the world is ultimately mechanical and machine-like and therefore acquiescent to the imposition of human purposes by way of engineering and the denomination of humanly constructed 'values'. Indeed, as Chesterton observed, all the towering materialisms of the modern age rest upon this single assumption.[30] Yet it is an assumption that, as Chesterton goes on to note, is almost certainly false. After all, what if the repetitive quality of natural order does not so much reflect its mechanical essence as it reflects God's joy in doing things again and again? Chesterton commented:

*more!*

But perhaps God is strong enough to exult in monotony. It is possible that God says every morning 'Do it again' to the sun; and every evening 'Do it again' to the moon. It may not be automatic necessity that makes all daisies alike; it may be that God makes every daisy separately, but has never got tired of making them. It may be that He has the eternal appetite of infancy; for we have sinned and grown old and our Father is younger than we. The repetition of nature may not be a mere recurrence; it may be a theatrical encore.[31]

Chesterton is only able to voice this possibility tentatively, for we simply do not know how God brings all things out of nothingness into being. Yet we do know by the testimony of the holy scriptures that God sustains the natural order of things because he *delights* in it and because he has pledged himself to sustain it for our sakes. 'As long as the earth endures', God promised Noah just prior to blessing him with increase and fruitfulness, 'seedtime and harvest, cold and heat, summer and winter, day and night will never cease' (Genesis 8:22).

Needless to say, this is wonderful! Indeed, it should inform all that we think and all that we do. For everything that is, everything that we are, everything that we are able to do, all of these are ultimately *the gifts of God*. This is why we are enjoined in Psalm 33 to sing songs of joy to the Lord, for he loves righteousness and justice, and the earth is full of his unfailing love. This is why Jesus tells us not to worry about our lives, about what we shall eat or drink or wear. And, finally, to cite just one further example of this critical biblical refrain, this is the simple recognition that the teacher in Ecclesiastes comes to, having considered the apparent vanity of human work in the world. He writes:

> Then I realized that it is good and proper for a man to eat and drink, and to find satisfaction in his toilsome labor under the sun during the few days of life God has given him – for this is his lot. Moreover, when God gives any man wealth and possessions, and enables him to enjoy them, to accept his lot and be

happy in his work – this is a gift of God. He seldom reflects on the days of his life, because God keeps him occupied with gladness of heart. (Ecclesiastes 5:18-20, NIV)

To say all of this is not to minimise the fact that the world often appears to be chaotic, anomic, and bent on the destruction of life. Indeed, the goodness and giftedness of existence might well have remained deeply ambiguous had the Christ not come and had the Father not raised him to life again on the first Easter morning. Yet the fact that God *did* raise Jesus from the dead assures us not simply that God continues to love the world that he has made but also that he has committed himself to redeeming it from its bondage to death and decay. This is the heart of the gospel of Jesus Christ, and it is what enables us now to speak confidently about the giftedness of being.

Yet the gift of the resurrected Christ also means that our attention must shift from the gift of the world to the Giver of this gift. For the resurrection does not simply assure us of the Father's continuing commitment to redeem this world but also that our destiny lies beyond it in 'the world to come'. Indeed, Jesus enjoins us to direct our attention beyond the things of this world to seek instead his Father's kingdom and 'his righteousness'. All of the things that we are so prone to worry about and that we assume we must somehow provide for ourselves, Jesus tells us, will indeed be given to us, but we must leave off worrying about them and pursuing them to follow him. Following him, he also says, means taking up the cross. Romanian theologian Dumitru Staniloae observed that:

> Without the cross man would be in danger of considering this world as the ultimate reality. Without the cross he would no longer see the world as God's gift. Without the cross the Son of God incarnate would have simply confirmed the image of the world as it is now as the final reality, and strictly speaking he could have been neither God nor God incarnate. The cross completes the fragmentary meaning of this world which has meaning when it is seen as the gift which has its value, but only a relative and not an absolute value.[32]

Our response to the gift of life, and particularly to the gift of new life in Christ, should be one of sheer *gratitude*. For gratitude is the only appropriate response to the receipt of any gift. Indeed, as Chesterton observed, gratitude is the true test of all happiness.[33] And don't we find that the words 'thank you' come almost involuntarily to our lips at those times when we are made aware of the beauty and deep goodness of things?

There is also a sense in which, having received the gift of the world, we are to respond by giving the things of the world back to God. In light of our earlier discussion of 'value', we might say that 'meaning' and 'purpose' are not so much built into the world of things – though the world has indeed been ordered by the divine wisdom – but that the things of the world ultimately *assume* meaning and *become* purposive through our free actions. Yet the things of the world do not become valuable simply because we desire them enough to place a 'value' on them – perhaps paying money for them – but rather because we use them in the service of *love*. Along with all of the other gifts we have been given, and as astonishing as this may sound, it seems that it has also been given to us in Christ to 'give' the world *back* to God in faithful and obedient service to his commands. Such an understanding has been developed theologically within Eastern Orthodoxy. As Staniloae observed:

> [T]he gifts given to us by God can become our gifts to God through the fact that we are free to give things back to God. We transform things into our gifts by the exercise of our freedom and by the love which we show to God. Towards this end we are able to transform and combine them endlessly. God has given the world to man not only as a gift of continuous fruitfulness, but as one immensely rich in possible alterations, actualized by each person through freedom and labour. This actualization, like the multiplication of talents given by God, is the gift of humankind to God.[34]

Finally we should respond to God's gracious gift of the world by simply being gracious and generous with one another. This is self-evidently good and right. What is perhaps less evident, however, is just how subversive generosity actually is of all that we have described under the heading of 'money culture'. The impact that money has had upon the bourgeois imagination, as we have seen, has been such as to have reduced all concrete qualities to quantities measured in prices. As a result of this, capitalist culture has become one in which more and more things are 'for sale', making the possession of money the final purpose for a great many people. In the kingdom of God, by contrast, *nothing* will be 'for sale' and *nothing* will be purchasable with money because everything will be freely given. The final purpose for the subjects of this kingdom will simply be *fellowship*. We get a glimpse of what this kingdom will be like in the early chapters of Acts, where we are told that, shortly after Pentecost, the believers had everything in common and sold their possessions and goods 'and gave to anyone as they had need'.[35] Such remarkable generosity should not be taken to reflect the early Christian community's passion for economic justice, for it was neither planned nor engineered, and there is no hint of political-economic ideology in the text. Rather this early Christian 'communism' seems simply to have been the spontaneous and, in a sense, natural reaction to the movement of God's Spirit within the community. Such a redemption of social order, I believe, is what we have to look forward to. Yet it is a reality we can anticipate now – 'in the mean time', as it were – by being gracious and generous with each other. As Ellul observed:

> In this new world we are entering, nothing is for sale; everything is given away. The mark of the world of money (where all is bought, where selling with all its consequences is the normal way to act) is the exact opposite of the mark of God's world where everything is free, where giving is the normal way to act. This is indeed different from our normal way of acting. This behavior is dictated by grace. Likewise the love created by money and by selling is the exact opposite of the love created by grace and by giving.[36]

Ellul went on to stress that we simply cannot overestimate the power of generosity in human relations. 'Not only does it destroy the power of money, but even more, it introduces the one who receives the gift into the world of grace ... and it begins a new chain of cause and effect which breaks the vicious cycle of selling and corruption.'[37] In short, gracious generosity is absolutely subversive of the power of money as 'mammon'.

## LIVING IN THE REAL WORLD

Does this mean that we cannot in good conscience continue to participate in the money economy? No, I do not think it means this at all, for the kingdom has not yet fully come. But this glimpse of redeemed social order does shed new light on our participation in the money economy, and it expands the horizons of economic rationality. For the *summum bonum* of this new kingdom ethic is not simply, as Weber put it with respect to the so-called Protestant ethic, 'the earning of more and more money, combined with the strict avoidance of all spontaneous enjoyment of life'. Rather it is the earning of money so that, as Paul wrote to the church in Corinth, we may have enough of everything and may provide in abundance for every good work (2 Corinthians 9:8). Of course, the new ethic is still disciplined in the sense that it takes economic rationality seriously, and it is still ascetic in the sense that it recognises and eschews the sins of covetousness and licentiousness, but it is not dour. On the contrary, it seeks simply to emulate the *graciousness* of God who, as the apostle James affirms, 'gives generously to all without finding fault' (James 1:5). Rather than producing the stern, almost wooden characters of Weberian analysis, the Christian ethic of money and possessions should, in addition to a disciplined and responsible work ethic, give rise to joyful and light-hearted generosity.

Paul's charge to the Corinthian believers recalls the eminently sensible advice John Wesley offered to his 18th-century parishioners concerning the use of money, advice that remains remarkably pertinent.[38] 'Gain all you can!' Wesley began – not, of course, at the expense of life or health, and not in such a way as to harm your neighbour, but simply using common sense and, as Wesley put it, 'using in your business all the understanding the God has given you', 'save all you can!' he continued. Don't waste what you have gained by fruitlessly trying to satisfy the desires of the flesh – which cannot be satisfied anyway – or by trying to win the fleeting and uncertain esteem of other people. What, after all, is the point of such effort? Doesn't it simply disclose fear and insecurity? Rather save what you make so that you can, and here Wesley completed the triad, 'Give all you can!' To grasp the reasons for this, Wesley continued:

> consider, when the Possessor of heaven and earth brought you into being, and placed you in this world ... He placed you here, not as a proprietor, but as a steward: as such, He entrusted you, for a season, with goods of various kinds; but the sole property of these still rests in Him, nor can ever be alienated from Him. As you yourself are not your own, but His, such is, likewise, all that you enjoy. Such is your soul and your body, not your own, but God's, and so is your substance in particular. And He has told you, in the most clear and express terms, how you are to employ it for Him, in such a manner, that it may be all an holy sacrifice, acceptable through Christ Jesus. And this light, easy service, He hath promised to reward with an eternal weight of glory.[39]

Interestingly, Wesley began his sermon on the use of money by citing the following passage from the Gospel of Luke: 'I say unto you, Make for yourselves friends of the mammon of unrighteousness; that, when ye fail, they may receive you into everlasting habitations.' The passage is taken from chapter 16 and it concludes what is often labelled 'The Parable of the Shrewd Steward'. I want to conclude my study by recounting the parable and commenting briefly on it. Jesus told his disciples:

There was a rich man whose manager was accused of wasting his possessions. So he called him in and asked him, 'What is this I hear about you? Give an account of your management, because you cannot be manager any longer.' The manager said to himself, 'What shall I do now? My master is taking away my job. I'm not strong enough to dig, and I'm ashamed to beg – I know what I'll do so that, when I lose my job here, people will welcome me into their houses.' So he called in each one of his master's debtors. He asked the first, 'How much do you owe my master?' 'Eight hundred gallons of olive oil,' he replied. The manager told him, 'Take your bill, sit down quickly, and make it four hundred.' Then he asked the second, 'And how much do you owe?' 'A thousand bushels of wheat,' he replied. He told him, 'Take your bill and make it eight hundred.' The master commended the dishonest manager because he had acted shrewdly. For the people of this world are more shrewd in dealing with their own kind than are the people of the light. I tell you, use worldly wealth to gain friends for yourselves, so that when it is gone, you will be welcomed into eternal dwellings. (Luke 16:1-9, NIV)

We are, it occurs to me, in essentially the same predicament as the manager in this parable. Like him, we are in trouble and we are aware that time is running out. Just as the manager was accused of wasting his master's possessions, we too are deeply implicated within a system that is problematical and undoubtedly at odds with our Master's desires for his creation in a great many respects. And yet we are also aware, just as the manager seems to have been, that we do not stand much of a chance outside this system, for not only have we come to depend upon its continuing productivity, but setting things entirely right lies far beyond our modest capabilities.

So what are we to do? Well, it seems to me that we ought to do the same thing that the shrewd steward in the parable did. We should continue to work within the market system – making friends of the 'mammon of unrighteousness' – but not for the sake of the system per se and not in such a way as to become captivated by the endlessly acquisitive 'spirit' of the system, but rather *subversively* and for the sake of ends that entirely transcend the system. Rather than working anxiously within the market system in the vain attempt to establish our own security for ourselves, we ought instead to *use* the system for the sake of *fellowship*, knowing full well that such is all that will survive into the world to come. After all, what other options are really open to us?

This, I think, is the answer to our initial question 'How should we think about capitalism?' I do not think we should be overly critical of the market system and neither should we be too concerned to defend it. Free market capitalism is a remarkably good system, but it is not perfect. The system has always stood and will always stand in need of moral valuation and discipline. Along this line, I believe we should *use* modern capitalism for the sake of our fellow servants, showing them grace, forgiving their debts, unexpectedly lightening their burdens, employing whatever wealth we have – wealth that we know we cannot keep for long – in the service of fellowship and friendship. And we should place our hope in the goodness and above all *in the graciousness of God*, the God for whom all things are possible.

# NOTES

Introduction
1   Jack Weatherford, *The History of Money: From Sandstone to Cyberspace* (New York: Three Rivers Press, 1997), 268.
2   Thomas L. Friedman, *The Lexus and the Olive Tree: Understanding Globalization* (New York: Anchor Books, 2000), 9.
3   Ibid., 53 ff.
4   Ibid., 9.
5   Ibid., 11.
6   Joseph A. Schumpeter, *Capitalism, Socialism and Democracy* (New York: Harper and Row, 1942; reprint, New York: Harper and Row, 1975), 83 (page citations are to the reprint edition; my emphasis).
7   Ibid.
8   Friedman, 11.
9   Ibid., 329.
10  Ibid., 364.
11  See, for example, Mike Featherstone, Scott Lash and Roland Robertson, eds, *Global Modernities*, Theory, Culture & Society Series (London: Sage, 1995).
12  Schumpeter, 123.
13  Ibid.
14  Michael Novak, *The Spirit of Democratic Capitalism* (New York: Simon & Schuster, 1982), 13.
15  See, for example, Craig M. Gay, 'The Intrinsic Secularity of Modern Economic Life,' in *The Way of the (Modern) World: Or Why It's Tempting to Live as if God Doesn't Exist* (Grand Rapid: Eerdmans, 1998), 131 ff.
16  Irving Kristol, *Two Cheers for Capitalism* (New York: Basic Books, 1978), 66.
17  Kurt Eichenwald, 'Could Capitalists Actually Bring Down Capitalism?' *New York Times*, 30 June 2002; sec. 4, pp. 1, 5.

18  Ibid., 5.

CHAPTER 1: SOURCES OF CAPITALISM'S REMARKABLE PRODUCTIVITY

1   Peter L. Berger, *The Capitalist Revolution: Fifty Propositions about Prosperity, Equality, & Liberty* (New York: Basic Books, 1986), 43.
2   Bjørn Lomborg, *The Skeptical Envirnomentalist: Measuring the Real State of the World* (Cambridge: Cambridge University Press, 2001), 50 ff.
3   Nathan Rosenberg and L. E. Birdzell, Jr., *How the West Grew Rich: The Economic Transformation of the Industrial World* (New York: Basic Books, 1986), 3.
4   Ibid.
5   Lomberg, 53.
6   Ibid., 59.
7   Ibid., 87.
8   Ibid., 65.
9   Ibid., 80-1.
10  Ibid., 82.
11  Ibid., 78.
12  Rosenberg and Birdzell, 3 (my emphasis).
13  'Over a year, or even over a decade, the economic gains, after allowing for the rise in population, were so little noticeable that it was widely believed that the gains were experienced only by the rich, and not by the poor. Only as the West's compounded growth continued through the twentieth century did its breadth become clear. It became obvious that Western working classes were increasingly well off and that the Western middle classes were prospering and growing as a proportion of the whole population. Not that poverty disappeared. The West's achievement was not the abolition of poverty but the reduction of its incidence from 90 percent of the population to 30 percent, 20 percent, or less, depending on the country and one's definition of poverty – a concept that seems to keep growing in content with economic growth itself. The continued expansion of Western economies through the twentieth century created an enormous gap between their wealth and the poverty from which they had escaped, but in which most of the world's people still live' (ibid., 6).
14  Ibid., 12 ff.
15  Ibid., 9.
16  Ibid., 12.
17  Ibid., 33.
18  Ibid., 20 ff.
19  Ibid., 33
20  Ibid., 33.
21  Ibid., 24.
22  Max Weber, *The Protestant Ethic and the Spirit of Capitalism* (New York: Charles Scribner's Sons, 1958), 68-69.
23  The following discussion of the Protestant Ethic thesis closely follows my analysis of the intrinsic secularity of modern economic life in Gay, 131 ff.
24  Weber, 171.
25  Ibid., 174.
26  Ibid., 108-9.
27  In the well-known study *Religion and the Rise of Capitalism: A Historical Study* (New York: Harcourt, Brace & Company, 1952), R. H. Tawney contended that

this freedom from tradition is clearly evident in Calvin's treatment of 'capital.' 'What [Calvin] did,' Tawney writes, 'was to change the plane on which the discussion was conducted, by treating the ethics of money-lending, not as a matter to be decided by an appeal to a special body of doctrine on the subject of usury, but as a particular case of the general problem of the social relations of a Christian community, which must be solved in the light of existing circumstances. The significant feature in his discussion of the subject is that he assumes credit to be a normal and inevitable incident in the life of society. He therefore dismisses the oft-quoted passages from the Old Testament and the Fathers as irrelevant, because [they were] designed for conditions which no longer exist, argues that the payment of interest for capital is as reasonable as the payment of rent for land, and throws on the conscience of the individual the obligation of seeing that it does not exceed the amount dictated by natural justice and the golden rule' (107-8).

28 Richard Baxter, cited in Weber, 162; also Tawney, 243.

29 Weber, 113-14.

30 Ibid., 115.

31 Of course, it is one thing to value practicality, as Baxter and the Puritans most cerainly did, but it is quite another to suggest that therefore the Puritans somehow sanctioned acquisitiveness, for they most certainly did not. Put somewhat differently, there is an obviously considerable difference between the Puritan stress upon working hard for the sake of the common good and the subsequent liberal assumption that in serving oneself one is thereby also automatically serving the common good. Indeed, with reference to the social-ethical teaching of the English Puritans between 1570 and 1640, Charles and Katherine George contended that this teaching was 'unreservedly anticapitalistic.' See Charles and Katherine George, 'Protestantism and Capitalism in Pre-Revolutionary England,' in *The Protestant Ethic and Modernization: A Comparative View*, ed., S. N. Eisenstadt (New York: Basic Books, 1968), 163. Rather, Puritan teaching explicitly condemned the continuous rational pursuit of wealth for its own sake, which, according to Weber, was the distinguishing characteristic of the spirit of modern capitalism.

Along similar lines, Leo Strauss observed that, while Weber's argument depended upon establishing a credible link between Puritanism and the view that held the limitless accumulation of capital to be an end in itself, he never actually established such a link. See Leo Strauss, 'Comment on the Weber Thesis Reexamined', *Church History* 30 (1961): 100-2. Strauss contended instead that the 'spirit' of modern capitalism actually originated in the political 'realism' of Machiavelli, which encouraged intellectuals to conceive of social order as being based upon socially useful passions or vices and not upon piety and virtue. 'Generally speaking,' Strauss notes, 'the Puritans were more open to the new philosophy or science both natural and moral than, e.g., Lutherans because Calvinism had broken with "pagan" philosophy (Aristotle) most radically; Puritanism was or became the natural *carrier* of a way of thinking which it had not originated in any way. By looking for the origin of the capitalist spirit in the way of thinking originated by Machiavelli one will also avoid an obvious pitfall of Weber's inquiry: Weber's study of the origin of the capitalist spirit is wholly unconcerned with the origins of the science of economics, for the science of economics is the authentic interpretation of the "capitalist spirit".' See also Leo

Strauss, *Natural Right and History* (Chicago: University of Chicago Press, 1950).

Along similar lines, John Milbank has suggested that purely secular social space only opened up as the Protestant reinterpretation of calling was united with the Reformers' anti-teleological epistemology. It was this combination that led to the modern belief that certain areas of social life are subject *only* to practical-rational assessment and manipulation. See John Milbank, *Theology and Social Theory: Beyond Secular Reason*, (Oxford: Basil Blackwell, 1990), 90.

The practical rationalisation of modern life may also have stemmed from the Puritan emphasis upon literacy and upon the rational formulation of doctrine. See Harry S. Stout, 'Puritanism Considered as a Profane Movement', in *Christian Scholar's Review* 10 (1980): 3-19. Or it may have issued from the insistence of post-Reformation sects upon the rights of individual conscience over and against state-sponsored churches, for this appears to have led to the formulation of the notion of individual 'rights'. See Guenther Roth, 'Religion and Revolutionary Beliefs: Sociological and Historical Dimensions in Max Weber's Work – In Memory of Ivan Vallier, 1927-1974', in *Social Forces* 12 (December): 255-72.

In short, Protestantism appears to have contributed to the practical and utilitarian temper of modern social life in a number of ways not specifically emphasized by Weber. In spite of all of the criticism and qualification of Weber's Protestant ethic thesis, however, it has undoubtedly served to draw attention to the intriguing similarities between seventeenth century Calvinism and the secular utilitarianism that would emerge a century later. As Alan Gilbert has noted, the difference between Puritanism's practical-rational commitment to mastering the world for the sake of God's kingdom, and the secular commitment to scientific mastery for the sake of rational 'progress' devolved, in practice, into little more than a slight difference in orientation. See Alan D. Gilbert, *The Making of Post-Christian Britain: A History of the Secularization of Modern Society*, (London: Longman, 1980), 33.

32    Historian Robert S. Michaelson shed interesting light on the evolution of later Puritanism in his essay 'Changes in the Puritan Concept of Calling or Vocation', in *New England Quarterly* 26 (1953): 315-36. Michaelson observed that in early Puritan understanding (*c.* 1600), one's 'particular vocation', or work in the world, was wholly circumscribed by one's 'general calling' to Christian faith and obedience. By the end of the seventeenth century, however, the Puritan understanding of the 'particular vocation' had been modified to suggest simply that it ought not to interfere with religious duties such as Sabbath observance. It was this subtle shift, Michaelson suggested, that eventually led to the secularisation of the notion of vocation. Michaelson also noted that this same period witnessed a subtle shift in the sorts of sins Puritan preachers were most concerned to censure. Whereas early Puritan divines had repeatedly denounced the sin of covetousness, later preachers focused most of their attention on the sins of sensuality, including those of laziness and idleness. In shifting attention to the sins of the flesh, however, the sins of the spirit, such as covetousness and ambition, were allowed a certain degree of latitude. In addition, by encouraging labor and industry as a way of avoiding fleshly indulgence, later Puritans came very close to blessing secular industry in and of itself and, by extension, the material wealth gained by this industry. Along this line, recall that only fifty years separate the England of Richard Baxter from the England of Wesley's famous lament (*c.* 1740) that 'wherever riches have increased, the essence of religion has decreased in the same proportion'. The Puritan sanctification of worldly vocations, Michaelson concluded,

was a significant boon to the developing commercialism of the late seventeenth century. 'The changes within the Puritan concept of vocation,' Michaelson wrote, 'prepared the way for significant and influential later developments. In England they helped produce Daniel Defoe's "complete English tradesman", whose religious life – it could be called that – was all but completely separated from his business. In America they contributed to the "wisdom" of Poor Richard as it came to be expressed in his almanacs and in *The Way to Wealth*. The separation between religion and business was completed with Poor Richard' (336).

In the English-speaking world, the most crucial figure in the devolution of Puritanism into secular utilitarianism was probably John Locke. More than anyone else, Locke was responsible for the amalgamation of Protestantism's affirmation of worldly work and the Cartesian ideal of disengaged and autonomous rationality. As Charles Taylor has noted in *Sources of the Self: The Making of the Modern Identity* (Cambridge: Harvard University Press, 1989), 242, while the Reformers had stressed living worshipfully before a Scripturally revealed God, Locke shifted the emphasis toward worshipping a naturally revealed God by living practically and rationally before Him. This was accomplished by means of a new, purportedly 'scientific', anthropology which stressed that the most important thing that needed to be said about human beings is that they are, like other creatures, oriented toward their own self-preservation. Locke Christianized this essentially secular view by insisting that this natural impulse toward self-preservation is actually providentially ordained and that Christians therefore served and pleased God by acting rationally and in the best interests of their own self-preservation. Already by the beginning of the eighteenth century, then, God was indeed believed to help those who helped themselves, and Lockean Christians helped themselves by acting practically and rationally to improve their own material circumstances.

Yet however the devolution of English Puritanism is recounted, the Protestant affirmation of worldly work by means of a redefinition of Christian 'calling' does appear to have suffered a kind of ironic reversal toward the end of the seventeenth century. While the Protestant understanding of calling had only been intended to refute the mistaken medieval distinction between 'sacred' and 'secular' work, and although the Reformers obviously had no intention of shifting the religious stress away from eternal life, this is what eventually happened. By the time of Locke (d. 1704), the Protestant affirmation of everyday life had come to mean the affirmation of the fundamental importance of the practical improvement of life in this world, whatever 'the world to come' might eventually hold in store. Indeed, the Christian religion itself came to be understood as chiefly a matter of the practical improvement of these worldly social conditions.

The radical implications of this relativization of eternal life over and against the practical exigencies of this life seem not to have been noticed at first. Locke, John Tolland and others simply assumed that Christian doctrine – at least to the extent that it was freed of the mysterious and superstitious elements with which it had become encrusted – *must* function in practice to improve human life, and that obedience to the Law of God must give rise to happiness here and now as well as, presumably, in the 'age to come'. But Lockean Christianity continued to devolve into Deism, and the requirements of human happiness altogether ceased to be determined theologically and came instead to be determined naturalistically and scientifically. Hence, as Taylor has noted, 'Locke helped to define and give currency to the growing Deist picture, which will emerge fully in the eighteenth century, of the universe as a vast interlocking order of beings, mutually subserving each other's flourishing, for whose design the architect of nature deserves our praise and thanks and admiration' (244). The Deist picture, with its stress upon reshaping the social world by means of practical-rational effort, subsequently became a kind of philosophical backdrop for *bourgeois* civilization. Indeed, apologies for market capitalism and for liberal democratic polity still most often presuppose just such a picture of the world.

Alasdair MacIntyre has also described the history of this devolution of the Christian moral tradition into modern liberal individualism in great detail (see especially *Whose Justice? Which Rationality?* (Notre Dame: University of Notre Dame Press, 1988). MacIntyre identifies David Hume as a key figure in this development, for he believes that it was due to the radical suspicion that Hume cast upon all substantive reasoning that it became increasingly difficult to question (or to discipline) an individual's desires or wants on the basis of any kind of substantive position.

33  Weber, 176.

34  Ibid., 53.

35  Tawney, 278-9. Tawney's thesis was that Puritanism paved the way for the practical rationalization of modern economic and social life by repudiating medieval Christian (Aristotelian) social ethics. Tawney observed, 'The shrewd, calculating commercialism which tries all human relations by pecuniary standards, the acquisitiveness which cannot rest while there are competitors to be conquered or profits to be won, the love of social power and hunger for economic gain – these irrepressible appetites had evoked from time immemorial the warnings and denunciations of saints and sages. Plunged in the cleansing waters of later Puritanism, the qualities which less enlightened ages had denounced as social vices emerged as economic virtues. They emerged as moral virtues as well. For the world exists not to be enjoyed, but to be conquered. Only its conqueror deserves the name of Christian' (248).

36  Berger, 107.

37  Ibid., 107-8.

38  Rosenberg and Birdzell, 'The Evolution of Institutions Favorable to Commerce', in *How the West Grew Rich*, 113-43. See also Hernando de Soto, *The Mystery of Capital: Why Capitalism Triumphs in the West and Falls Everywhere Else* (New York: Basic Books, 2000).

39  Lewis Mumford, *Technics and Civilization* (London: Routledge & Sons, 1934), 46-7.

40  Ibid., 47.

41  Robert Doede, 'The Decline of Anthropomorphic Explanation: From Animism to Deconstructionism' (an unpublished paper delivered to the Regent College Faculty, Vancouver, BC, 1992).

42  Rosenberg and Birdzell, 33.

43  Bruce G. Carruthers and Wendy Nelson Espeland, 'Accounting for Rationality: Double-Entry Bookkeeping and the Rhetoric of Economic Rationality,' in *American Journal of Sociology* 97 (July 1991): 57.

44  Georg Simmel, *The Philosophy of Money*, trans. Tom Bottomore and David Frisby (London: Routledge & Kegan Paul, 1978), 211.

45  See Weatherford, *The History of Money* and Jonathan Williams, ed., *Money: A*

*History* (New York: St Martin's Press, 1997).

46  Schumpeter, 123.

47  Ibid.

48  Novak, 99.

49  Simmel, 232.

50  Donald N. Levine, 'Rationality and Freedom: Weber and Beyond', in *Sociological Inquiry* 51 (1981): 5-25.

51  Berger, 110.

52  Ferdinand Toennies, *Community and Association* (London: Routledge & Kegan Paul, 1955).

53  Robert L. Heilbroner, *The Worldly Philosphers: The Lives, Times, and Ideas of the Great Economic Thinkers*, 7th ed. (New York: Simon & Schuster, 1999).

54  Ibid., 20.

55  Ibid., 21.

56  Berger, 43.

57  Novak, 14.

58  Ibid.

59  Berger, 81.

60  Ibid., 84.

61  Alexis de Tocqueville, *Democracy in America*, trans. George Lawrence (Garden City, New York: Doubleday & Co., 1969).

62  Ibid., 429.

63  Ibid., 462.

64  Ibid., 615.

65  Ibid., 645.

CHAPTER 2: UNINTENDED CONSEQUENCES OF CAPITALISM'S 'EXALTATION OF THE MONETARY UNIT'

1  Georg Simmel, 'The Metropolis and Mental Life', in *The Sociology of Georg Simmel*, trans. and ed. Kurt H. Wolff (New York: The Free Press, 1950), 414.

2  Berger, 43.

3  Ibid., 81.

4  Novak, 13.

5  Ibid., 359-60.

6  Peter L. Berger, *Pyramids of Sacrifice: Political Ethics and Social Change* (Garden City, NY: Anchor Books, 1974), 23.

7  See also Tage Lindbom, *The Myth of Democracy* (Grand Rapids: Eerdmans, 1996). '[U]nbridled liberty ...,' Lindbom observes, 'dissolves all ideas of value, it relativizes and atomizes. In the life of secularized man as well as in secularized society, strivings for liberty always open up new and growing sectors of pluralism and relativism at the expense of stability and continuity of values. Endless dialogue, debate, and scientific investigation fill the vacuum' (71).

8  Francis Fukuyama, 'The End of History?' in *The National Interest* (Summer 1989): 3-18.

9  Ibid., 4.

10  Ibid., 8.

11  Ibid., 18.

12  Ibid.

13  See Leo Strauss, 'An Introduction to Heideggarian Existentialism', in *The Rebirth*

*of Classical Political Rationalism: An Introduction to the Thought of Leo Strauss*, ed. Thomas L. Pangle (Chicago: University of Chicago Press, 1989), 42.

14  Weber, 182.

15  Friedrich Nietzsche, *Thus Spake Zarathustra: A Book for None and All*, trans. Walter Kaufmann (New York, Penguin, 1966), 17-18.

16  Tocqueville, 645.

17  José Ortega y Gassett, *The Revolt of the Masses* (New York: Mentor, 1932).

18  Ibid., 31-2.

19  Novak, 55.

20  Harold J. Laski, *The Rise of European Liberalism: An Essay in Interpretation* (London: Unwin Books, 1936; reprint, London: Unwin Books, 1962), 21-2 (page citations are to the reprint edition).

21  Joseph Cropsey, 'Adam Smith', in *History of Political Philosophy*, 3rd edition, eds Leo Strauss & Joseph Cropsey (Chicago: University of Chicago Press, 1987), 652.

22  James Boswell, 'Life of Samuel Johnson (1791)', cited in *The Oxford Dictionary of Quotations*, ed. Elizabeth Knowles, 5th ed. (Oxford: Oxford University Press, 1999), 414:24.

23  Novak, 62.

24  Weber, 17.

25  Robert A. Nisbet, *Community and Power* (Oxford: Oxford University Press, 1962), 239-40.

26  Berger, *Capitalist Revolution*, 221.

27  John Wesley, cited in Weber, 175.

28  Alasdair MacIntyre, *After Virtue: A Study in Moral Theory*, 2nd ed. (Notre Dame: University of Notre Dame Press, 1984).

29  Ibid., 196.

30  Neil Postman, *Technopoly: The Surrender of Culture to Technology* (New York: Vintage, 1993), 14.

31  Ibid., 20, though Postman is not concerned to make such points about money but rather about modern technology generally.

32  Karl Marx, cited in Mumford, 23-4.

33  Schumpeter, 127.

34  Ibid.

35  Ibid., 126.

36  Ibid.

37  Ibid., 142.

38  Ibid.

39  Ibid., 61.

40  Robert Nisbet, *The Present Age: Progress and Anarchy in Modern America* (New York: Harper & Row, 1988), 84 ff.

41  Ibid., 87.

42  Ibid., 91.

43  Tom Bottomore and David Frisby, 'Introduction to the Translation', in Simmel, *Philosophy of Money*, 15.

44  Simmel, *Philosophy of Money*, 211.

45  Ibid., 232.

46  Ibid. 'The tremendous and wide-reaching power of the process by which money is elevated from its intermediary position to absolute importance,' Simmel notes,

'is best illuminated by the fact that the negation of its meaning [as in voluntary poverty] is elevated to the identical form [i.e., the highest purpose]' (*Philosophy of Money*, 254).

47  Ibid., 354.
48  Ibid., 296.
49  Ibid., 346.
50  Berger, *Capitalist Revolution*, 113.
51  Simmel, *Philosophy of Money*, 448.
52  Simmel, 'The Metropolis and Mental Life', 412.
53  Simmel, *Philosophy of Money*, 256.
54  Ibid., 256.
55  Simmel, 'Metropolis and Mental Life', 414.
56  Ibid.
57  Simmel, *Philosophy of Money*, 257.
58  Ibid., 484.
59  Christopher Dawson, *Progress and Religion: An Historical Inquiry* (Peru, IL: Sherwood Sugden & Co., 1991), 228.
60  Karl Marx and Friedrich Engels, 'The Communist Manifesto', in *Essential Works of Marxism*, ed. Arthur P. Mendel (New York: Bantam Books, 1961), 16.
61  Simmel, 'Metropolis and Mental Life', 414.
62  Simmel, *Philosophy of Money*, 485.
63  Søren Kierkegaard, *The Present Age & Of the Difference Between a Genius and an Apostle*, trans. Alexander Dru (New York: Harper & Row, 1962), 40-1.
64  Glenn Tinder, *The Political Meaning of Christianity: The Prophetic Stance* (San Francisco: HarperSanFrancisco, 1989), 184.
65  Simmel, *Philosophy of Money*, 236.
66  Ibid.

CHAPTER 3:  AN ECONOMY OF SHREWD STEWARDSHIP
1  Robert Bellah, 'The Triumph of Capitalism – Or the Rise of Market Totalitarianism', *New Oxford Review* 58 (March 1991): 8-15.
2  George Grant, 'In Defense of North America', in *Technology and Empire: Perspectives on North America* (Toronto: Anansi, 1969), 17.
3  Ibid., 40.
4  Berger, *Capitalist Revolution*, 113.
5  Robert Goudzwaard, *Capitalism and Progress: A Diagnosis of Western Society* (Grand Rapids: Eerdmans, 1979).
6  Ibid., 112.
7  Tocqueville, 430.
8  Carl L. Becker, *The Heavenly City of the Eighteenth Century Philosophers* (New Haven: Yale University Press, 1932), 27-8.
9  Ibid., 28.
10  Steven Seidman, *Liberalism and the Origins of European Social Theory* (Berkeley: University of California Press, 1983), 39.
11  Ibid.
12  Novak, 43.
13  Romano Guardini, *Letters from Lake Como: Explorations in Technology and the Human Race* (Grand Rapids: Eerdmans, 1994), 71-2.
14  Sadly, living organisms don't often survive the process of scientific objectification.

Indeed, things must often actually be killed before they can be known in this modern way. See Mumford, 304-5.

15 H. H. Gerth and C. W. Mills, *From Max Weber* (New York: Oxford University Press, 1946), 139.

16 Grant, 35.

17 Martin Buber, *I and Thou*, trans. Walter Kaufmann (New York: Charles Scribner's Sons, 1970).

18 Ibid., 110.

19 G. K. Chesterton, *The Everlasting Man* (Garden City, NY: Doubleday & Co., 1955), 149.

20 Ibid., 152.

21 Ibid., 152-3.

22 Ibid., 153.

23 Glenn Tinder, *Against Fate: An Essay on Personal Dignity*, Loyola Lecture Series in Personal Analysis, ed. Richard Shelley Hartigan (Notre Dame, IN: University of Notre Dame Press, 1981), 9.

24 See Leo Strauss, *An Introduction to Political Philosophy: Ten Essays by Leo Strauss* (Detroit: Wayne State University Press, 1989), 84.

25 Jacques Ellul, *Money and Power* (Grand Rapids: Eerdmans, 1984), 81.

26 Ibid., 81.

27 Ibid., 76.

28 Richard John Neuhaus, 'Wealth and Whimsy: On Economic Creativity', in *First Things* (August/September 1990): 23-30.

29 Ibid., 29.

30 G. K. Chesterton, *Orthodoxy* (Garden City, NY: Doubleday & Co., 1959), 60.

31 Ibid.

32 Dumitru Staniloae cited in Charles Miller, *The Gift of the World: An Introduction to the Theology of Dumitru Staniloae* (Edinburgh: T. & T. Clark, 2000), 79.

33 Chesterton, *Orthodoxy*, 55.

34 Staniloae cited in Miller, 62.

35 Acts 2:44-45.

36 Ellul, 112.

37 Ibid.

38 John Wesley, 'The Use of Money', in *On Moral Business: Classical and Contemporary Resources for Ethics in Economic Life*, ed. Max Stackhouse, Dennis P. McCann, Shirley J. Roels, & Preston N. Williams (Grand Rapids, MI: Eerdmans, 1995), 193-7.

39 Ibid., 196.

CPSIA information can be obtained at www.ICGtesting.com
Printed in the USA
LVOW050513240712

291231LV00001B/34/A

9 780802 827753